P9-EMQ-340

RIPPOWAM CISQUA SCHOOL LIBRARY

Rippowam Campus, Box 488, Bedford, N. Y. 10506

970.4
YOU

20300764

The First Americans
* * * * * * * * * * * * * * *

INDIANS OF THE ARCTIC AND SUBARCTIC

Paula Younkin

RIPPOWAM CISQUA SCHOOL LIBRARY

Rippowam Campus, Box 488, Bedford, N. Y. 10506

Facts On File, Inc.

AN INFOBASE HOLDINGS COMPANY

About *The First Americans* Series:

This eight-volume series presents the rich and varied cultures of the many Native American tribes, placing each within its geographical and historical context. Each volume covers a different cultural area, providing an understanding of all the major North American Indian tribes in a systematic, region-by-region survey. The series emphasizes the contributions of Native Americans to American culture, illustrating their legacy in striking photographs within the text and in all-color photo essays.

Indians of the Arctic and Subarctic

Copyright © 1992 by Benford Books, Inc.

All rights reserved. No part of this book may be reproduced or utilized in any form or by any means, electronic or mechanical, including photocopying, recording, or by any information storage or retrieval systems, without permission in writing from the publisher. For information contact:

Facts On File, Inc.
11 Penn Plaza
New York NY 10001

Library of Congress Cataloging-in-Publication Data

Younkin, Paula
    Indians of the Arctic and Subarctic / Paula Younkin
       p.   cm. — The First Americans series
    Includes index.
    Summary: Examines the history, culture, changing fortunes, and
current situation of the various Indian peoples of Canada, Alaska, and Greenland.
    ISBN 0-8160-2391-3
      1. Indians of North America—Canada—Juvenile literature.
      2. Indians of North America—Arctic regions—Juvenile literature.
      3. Indians of North America—Alaska—Juvenile literature.
      4. Indians of North America—Greenland—Juvenile literature.
      5. Indians of North America—Alaska—Juvenile literature.
    [1. Indians of North America—Canada. 2. Indians of North America—Arctic regions.
3. Indians of North America—Alaska. 4. Eskimos.]
    I. Title   II. Series.
    E78.C2Y84   1991
    998'.00497—dc20   90–47675

Facts On File books are available at special discounts when purchased in bulk quantities for businesses, associations, institutions or sales promotions. Please call our Special Sales Department in New York at 212/967-8800 or 800/322-8755.

Design by Carmela Pereira
Jacket design by Donna Sinisgalli
Typography & composition by Tony Meisel
Manufactured in MEXICO

10 9 8 7 6 5 4 3 2

This book is printed on acid-free paper.

▲ An Inuit family is dressed for the Arctic winter in double-layered parkas. Fur on the outside layer sheds snow, while fur on the inside layer traps body heat next to the skin.

CONTENTS

* * * * * * * * * * * * * * *

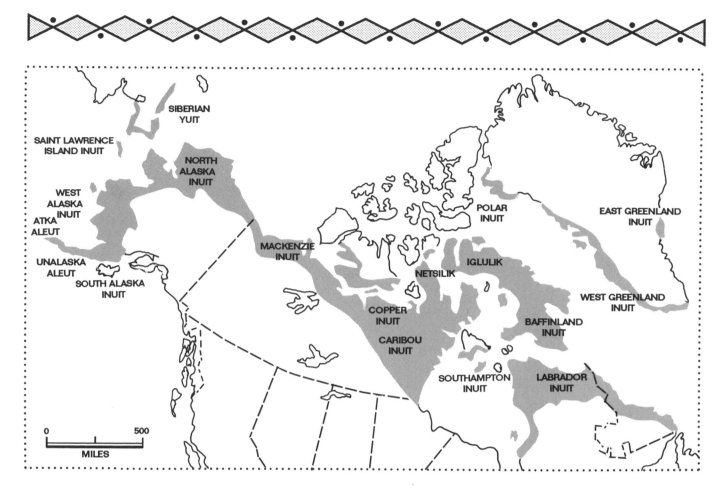

SIBERIAN
YUIT

SAINT LAWRENCE
ISLAND INUIT

NORTH
ALASKA
INUIT

WEST
ALASKA
INUIT
ATKA
ALEUT

MACKENZIE
INUIT

POLAR
INUIT

EAST GREENLAND
INUIT

UNALASKA
ALEUT

SOUTH ALASKA
INUIT

NETSILIK

IGLULIK

WEST GREENLAND
INUIT

COPPER
INUIT

BAFFINLAND
INUIT

CARIBOU
INUIT

SOUTHAMPTON
INUIT

LABRADOR
INUIT

0   500
MILES

THE ARCTIC CULTURE AREA

The approximate traditional tribal boundaries of the Arctic culture area are shown in the larger map, with modern state boundaries. The smaller map shows the culture area in relation to all of North America.

THE SUBARCTIC CULTURE AREA

The approximate traditional tribal boundaries of the Sub-arctic culture area are shown in the larger map, with modern state boundaries. The smaller map shows the culture area in relation to all of North America.

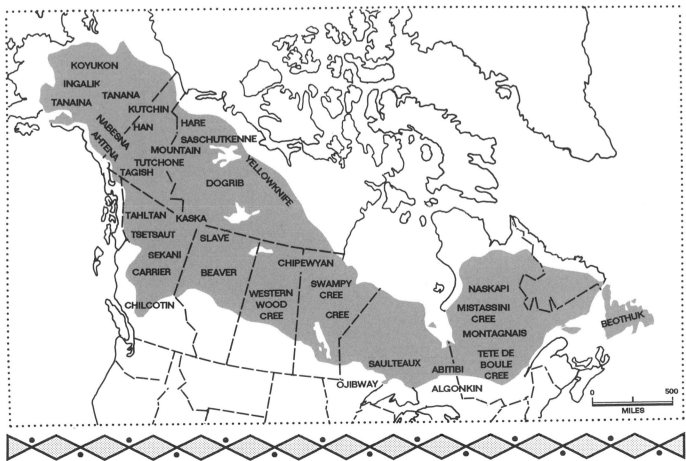

KOYUKON
INGALIK
TANAINA TANANA
KUTCHIN
NABESNA HAN HARE
AHTENA SASCHUTKENNE
MOUNTAIN
TUTCHONE YELLOWKNIFE
TAGISH
DOGRIB
TAHLTAN KASKA
TSETSAUT SLAVE
SEKANI CHIPEWYAN
CARRIER BEAVER
WESTERN SWAMPY NASKAPI
WOOD CREE
CHILCOTIN CREE MISTASSINI
CREE
MONTAGNAIS BEOTHUK
TETE DE
SAULTEAUX BOULE
ABITIBI CREE
OJIBWAY ALGONKIN

0   500
MILES

▲ An Inuit maker of spears and lances proudly shows his work in this photograph from 1935.

CHAPTER ONE

* * * * * * * * * * * * * *

ROOTS

he original peoples of the North American Arctic and Subarctic might be called the *survivors*—a word that takes on special meaning when applied to those people who made their home in the cruelest climate on Earth. But the term *survive* does not adequately convey the enormity of their achievement. Of all the peoples in the history of the world, they were among the toughest, most resourceful, and most adaptable.

While surviving, they developed culturally rich lifeways in spiritual harmony with nature. They lived and traveled in hunting bands that moved with the seasons and the animals on which their lives depended. Most of their activities centered on staying warm and getting food—a constant struggle—yet their cultures reflect a deep respect for nature, rather than a sense of desperation. Their everyday tools and utensils—such as boats, harpoons, knives, snowshoes, and baskets—were often so exquisitely crafted that modern people view them as works of art.

Frequently, native peoples of the Subarctic and Arctic are referred to simply as Eskimos and Indians. Those designations overlook the fact that the Subarctic and Arctic natives comprise four distinct cultural groupings: the Eskimo, Aleut, Athapascan, and Algonquian.

The four groupings are determined by the languages they speak. The Athapascan of the Subarctic, for example, are linguistically related to the Indians who migrated to the American Southwest. While they too are Athapascan, their lifeways are adapted to a hot climate. The Athapascan who migrated into the Subarctic and Arctic regions have more in common with the Eskimo than with their southwestern relatives. Yet they, like each of the Subarctic and Arctic groups, are a proud and culturally unique people. The Subarctic Athapascan now call their homeland the Dene Nation and prefer to be called *Dene* (pronounced *Dinnie*), meaning "people" or "person."

The Eskimo are composed of two linguistic groups, the Inuit and the Yuit. The word *Eskimo* may come from a name that the Algonquian Indians mockingly called their neighbors, meaning "eaters of raw meat." The Eskimo prefer their own name *Inuit*, meaning "the People." Therefore, from here on, the native peoples of the Arctic and Subarctic regions of North America will be refered to as the Inuit, the Yuit, the Aleut, the Dene, and the Algonquian. The Aleut, Dene, Yuit, and Algonquian people can collectively be called Indians; they are also called natives.

▲ An Inuit woman sits in front of her summer skin tent at Point Barrow, Alaska. In summer, Inuit families moved to coastal areas to fish and hunt seal.

CULTURAL AREAS

The Arctic cultural area of North America spans 5,000 miles, from the eastern Siberian coast of the Soviet Union in the west, across Canada, to the eastern coast of Greenland in the east. It lies both above and below the Arctic Circle, including the Aleutian Islands off the southwest coast of Alaska. In Canada, the Arctic cultural area includes the region surrounding the northern half of Hudson Bay and extends down the southern coast of Labrador to its southernmost point.

The Subarctic cultural area spreads across most of the interior of Alaska and Canada, beginning in the west at Cook Inlet on the Pacific Ocean and continuing east to include Newfoundland. Its northern boundary lies just inside the Arctic Circle in the west, then drops south, following the southwestern coast of Hudson Bay, continuing around James Bay, and bordering the Arctic cultural areas of Quebec and Labrador. The southern boundary is less definite, but it ends approximately in the parts of southern Canada where the Plains and Plateau cultural areas begin.

The Inuit and the Aleut are usually thought of as the Arctic peoples, while the Dene and Algonquian are considered Subarctic peoples. However, *cultural* and *geographical* regions are not the same. Geographical regions are determined by location; cultural areas are determined by a people's lifeways and languages. Because *where* people live has a great deal to do with *how* they live, cultural and geographical regions tend to overlap. For example, the territories of the Hare and Kutchin Indians, two Dene groups, lie partly within the Arctic Circle. More than half of the Inuit and Yuit groups—the South Alaska Inuit and the Copper Inuit, for example—live *below* the Arctic Circle, or in the Subarctic.

PARKAS

The hooded parkas people wear today originated with the Inuit. The Inuit were expert at keeping warm in a very cold climate. The woman shown here has lip ornaments, or labrets, of ivory under her lower lip.

▲ An eagle design adorns this ivory-handled war knife made by a Tahltan.

SHARED LIFEWAYS

The Subarctic and Arctic natives were primarily hunters. All the groups also fished, although some did more than others, depending on their location. To a lesser extent they were gatherers, meaning they supplemented their diets with plants. The Algonquian living near Lake Superior were able to gather wild rice and collect maple syrup, as well as trade with Indians farther south for corn and tobacco. Those luxuries, however, were not within reach of people living in the chilly northern Subarctic and Arctic areas.

As vegetation grew more sparse going north, the people depended more on animals for food and warmth. Animal skins were the materials for clothing, blankets, and tents, and animal fat was the fuel that provided heat. Where wood was not available, bones, antlers, and hides were primary materials for building and for making tools and hunting equipment.

People's time was given mostly to making hunting gear, hunting, and processing the meat and hides when hunting was successful. Theirs was a schedule that did not allow for organized, large-scale warfare. However, tensions existed between various groups whose territories bordered each other. For example, the Dene, who were not known for being warlike, had occasional violent encounters with the Inuit to the north and with the Cree, an Algonquian group, to the south. Suspicions and hostilities possibly stemmed from prejudices between peoples whose lifeways and appearance were different. The deadly attacks on each other fueled more bad feeling and violence.

Warfare usually took the form of raids and sneak attacks. Violence between Inuit groups was often prompted by an ancient feud, or revenge for the murder of a relative, or for illness believed to be caused by sorcery practiced by someone in another band. Instances of violence between Dene groups were usually for revenge or to kidnap women. Overall, however, the various Subarctic and Arctic peoples shared the land in cautious peace and were, in many instances, on friendly terms.

The inclination to share was far more characteristic of the Subarctic and Arctic peoples than the tendency to make war. They regarded the land and its resources as gifts to be used and shared, not possessed and hoarded. Times of famine were inevitable, and people prepared for scarcity by freezing and drying meat. Even so, winter often outlasted the food supplies, and starvation became a reality. When famine struck, people would share their last bite of food, not knowing when they might eat again. Sharing and cooperation characterized family and tribal relationships among all groups of the Subarctic and Arctic.

ORIGINS

Scientists theorize that the people who first made their lives in the Arctic and Subarctic migrated from Eurasia into North America over a land bridge, called Beringia, that had connected Siberia and Alaska. The land bridge existed only during periods of wide-spread glaciation, when ice causes sea levels to drop as much as 300 feet. Between ice ages, Beringia is the floor of the Bering Sea.

The Algonquian natives of the southeastern Subarctic may be descendents of the earliest arrivals, hunting bands who came by foot over the land bridge 19,000 to 27,000 years ago. The migrant ancestors of the Aleut possibly date back to 6,000 B.C. or even earlier.

The Inuit and Dene natives are believed to be descendants of people who migrated into North America between 3,000 and 1,000 B.C. By then the land bridge had disappeared again under water, and so archaeologists believe these "newcomers" crossed the 56 miles between the continents in skin boats and wooden dugouts (boats made by hollowing out logs).

PHYSICAL CHARACTERISTICS

Members of all native groups of the Arctic and Subarctic share some physical traits, such as dark eyes, straight black hair, and swarthy complexions. But the Inuit and Indians are also physically distinct from each other in some ways. The eyes of the Inuit have an *epicanthic eyefold*—the skin of the upper eyelid folds over the inner angle of the eye, creating a slanted appearance. In general, the shape of their faces is round and flat, with small noses; the Indians' faces have more angular lines and prominent noses. The Inuit also tend to be lighter skinned and shorter than Indians.

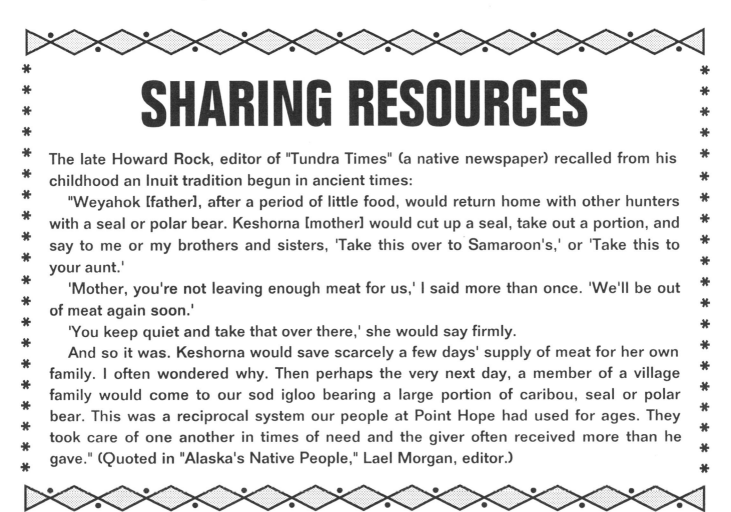

SHARING RESOURCES

The late Howard Rock, editor of "Tundra Times" (a native newspaper) recalled from his childhood an Inuit tradition begun in ancient times:

"Weyahok [father], after a period of little food, would return home with other hunters with a seal or polar bear. Keshorna [mother] would cut up a seal, take out a portion, and say to me or my brothers and sisters, 'Take this over to Samaroon's,' or 'Take this to your aunt.'

'Mother, you're not leaving enough meat for us,' I said more than once. 'We'll be out of meat again soon.'

'You keep quiet and take that over there,' she would say firmly.

And so it was. Keshorna would save scarcely a few days' supply of meat for her own family. I often wondered why. Then perhaps the very next day, a member of a village family would come to our sod igloo bearing a large portion of caribou, seal or polar bear. This was a reciprocal system our people at Point Hope had used for ages. They took care of one another in times of need and the giver often received more than he gave." (Quoted in "Alaska's Native People," Lael Morgan, editor.)

TRIBAL GROUPINGS

The word *band* is a more accurate term than *tribe* to describe the groupings of natives of the sparsely populated Arctic and Subarctic. Bands are more typical of hunting groups who are always on the move. They are less permanent than tribes and their leaders serve only as long as the band stays together. Tribal chiefs, on the other hand, often hold their position for life.

SOCIAL ORGANIZATION

In the Subarctic and Arctic, families formed bands for a specific purpose, usually for hunting or gathering food. They chose their leaders—often a highly skilled hunter—on the basis of his (the leader was almost always a man) personal merit and knowledge. In fact, an Inuit word for a person of authority is *isumatag*, meaning "one who thinks."

Families in the band relied on the leader to know when to move and how food should be divided. The leader served as long as the band stayed together, usually until the end of a hunt-

▲ The Native Americans of the Subarctic region preserved fish by drying it on frames such as this one, which is set up in front of a tepee. A good summer catch helped a family survive the hard winter.

ing cycle, and then families would go their own ways.

Even though social and political organization among Arctic and Subarctic natives was typically informal and temporary, marriage and kinship between bands strengthened cooperative relationships. In some native groups, tribal feeling was stronger than in others and extended beyond family ties. Two Dene groups, the Kutchin and the Slave, represent the two different attitudes.

The Kutchin had a strong sense of tribal identity. Unlike other Dene groups, the Kutchin further organized themselves by clans, or extended families. The Slave, on the other hand, lived in separate, scattered groups. They had no name for themselves and did not see themselves as belonging to a band or tribe. The Cree, an Algonquian group, called them *Awokanak*, meaning "timid people," or slaves; the Beaver, another Dene group, called them *Tsade*, also meaning "timid

▲ Dogrib Indians, a Dene tribe, set out in canoes on Great Slave Lake in Canada's Northwest Territory. Each Dene tribe had its individual style of canoe.

people." The name *Slave* was given them after contact with Europeans who called them *Slaveys*, possibly in a failed attempt to pronounce the word *Tsade*.

THE LAND

The Arctic and Subarctic are two distinct geographic regions, but in both severe cold lasts much of the year. The early pioneers of the Arctic had to be technologically advanced on arrival, bringing with them the special knowledge and skills to stay warm and find food. Those who could not moved on or fell victim to the savage Arctic climate.

The Arctic region lies north of the Rockies, within the Arctic Circle, and borders on three oceans—the Pacific, the Atlantic, and the Arctic. Its two million square miles of rolling, desertlike plains, called the *tundra*, lies north of the tree-

line. (The *treeline* is the natural division between the Arctic and the Subarctic regions, or the northernmost point above which trees can no longer grow due to ground frost and freezing Arctic winds.) The tundra is characterized by dwarf and low-growing plants during the short growing season.

Most of the year, however, the tundra looks as if it were made of snow and ice, even though annual rainfall scarcely reaches 10 inches. Extreme cold keeps the snow from melting, and powerful winds create blizzards and snowdrifts that can bury houses. Arctic winters are long and dark. The Polar Inuit living in the northernmost settlements of Greenland do not see the sun from late October to mid-February.

As spring approaches in the Arctic, the pack ice, a dense mass of sea ice formed when huge chunks of ice are crushed or packed together, begins to thaw and break up into floes. Near the North Pole, the pack ice never melts, while closer to the Arctic coastline it expands and recedes with the seasons.

The melting turns the tundra into an immense, boggy landscape of lakes and ponds. Wa-

SUBARCTIC GROUPS

The Indian groups, or tribes, of the Subarctic form two major groupings—Dene in the west and Algonquian in the east. Within each of these two regional groupings are tribes, each with its own dialect and customs. (The one exception to these two groupings is the Beothuk of Newfoundland, who speak Beothukan, a language unrelated to any other Indian language.)

DENE GROUPS

WESTERNMOST	EAST OF THE CANADIAN ROCKIES	NEAR GREAT BEAR LAKE/ GREAT SLAVE LAKE
Koyukon	Tahltan	Hare
Kutchin	Tutchone	Dogrib
Ingalik	Tsetsaut	Slave
Tanana	Mountain	Beaver
Tanaina	Sekani	Yellowknife
Ahtena	Carrier	Chipewyan
Nabesna	Chilcotin	Saschutkenne
Han	Tagish	
	Kaska	

ALGONQUIAN GROUPS

WESTERN	EASTERN
Western Wood Cree	Mistassini Cree
Swampy Cree	Tete de Boule Cree
Cree	Montagnais
	Naskapi
	northern Ojibway
	Saulteaux
	Abitibi

BEOTHUKAN GROUP

Beothuk

▲ These Alaska Inuit are dressed in the comfortable, heat-conserving fur clothing first designed by their early ancestors. The men, women, and children in this photograph from 1894 have typical Inuit features: a round, somewhat flat face and eyes that are characterized by an epicanthic eyefold.

ter from the melted ice collects on the surface because it cannot drain or soak into the permanently frozen earth, or *permafrost*, that is just below the surface soil.

In the summer, the tundra comes to life with vegetation. Herbs, grasses, dwarf shrubs, lichens, scrub brush, spongy mosses, spinachlike greens, ferns, wild celery, and a wide variety of berries all sprout up. In some areas a blaze of wildflowers thrives in the endless sunlight.

By mid-August, however, the temperature drops again and the days grow shorter. Skies turn steely gray and whiteouts occur—a polar weather condition in which nothing casts a shadow and only the faint outlines of dark objects are visible. The horizon is hidden from view, and a person loses all sense of distance and direction. By September, the open water begins to freeze, and sources of fresh water become scarce.

The Subarctic is the zone just south of the Arctic Circle, beginning at the treeline and ex-

ARCTIC GROUPS

The chart below lists the regional groups found in the Arctic. Several Inuit and Yuit groups, as well as the Aleut, do not live in the Arctic Circle. Those who do not are noted with an asterisk.

ALEUT, INUIT, AND YUIT GROUPS

ALEUT	ALASKA	CENTRAL	GREENLAND
Atka Aleut*	North Alaska Inuit	Netsilik	East Greenland Inuit*
Unalaska Aleut*	West Alaska Inuit	Iglulik	West Greenland Inuit*
	South Alaska Inuit*	Caribou Inuit*	Polar Inuit
	St. Lawrence Island Inuit	Copper Inuit*	
	Siberian Yuit	Southampton Inuit*	
	Mackenzie Inuit*	Baffinland Inuit*	
		Labrador Inuit*	

Each regional group is composed of other villages and bands. For example, the Alaska Inuit and Yuit include 21 distinct tribes, such as the Malemiut, Kingikmiut, and Tareumiut (the suffix "-miut" means people).

tending south. This region is characterized by woodlands called the *taiga*. The taiga consists largely of boreal forests—coniferous (cone-bearing) trees such as spruce, pine, and fir, as well as aspen, tamarack, alder, willow, and birch trees. As one travels south in the Subarctic, the forests grow taller and denser.

The coasts of Alaska and eastern Canada get heavy rains and snows, and even the drier inland region has a wealth of water—ponds, swamps, bogs, and streams as well as huge lakes and powerful rivers. Although the climate is more varied than in the Arctic, the Subarctic winters are generally long, severe, and white.

Summers in the Subarctic tend to be cool and short, lasting from six weeks to three months, depending on the location. While short summers and permafrost make agriculture impossible in the Arctic, some hardy vegetables, such as carrots, turnips, peas, and beans, can be grown in the southernmost parts of the Subarctic.

LANGUAGES

The languages of the Arctic and Subarctic native peoples are grouped into four linguistic families: Eskimo-Aleut or "Eskaleut" (spoken by the Aleut and the Inuit); Yupik (spoken by the Yuit); Dene; and Algonquian. Within each linguistic family are several related languages, and each of those languages is composed of several dialects. For instance, there is no *one* Inuit language, even though Inuit from different regions can usually understand each other.

A North Alaska Inuit and a Polar Inuit in Greenland, however, may have some difficulty communicating, as might Dene or Algonquian from different tribes. A Swampy Cree and a Naskapi, both Subarctic Indians whose languages belong to the Algonquian family, might need an interpreter to converse with each other.

Each language tells much about the culture of its speakers. For example, the Central Inuit have approximately 70 words for snow, because for them, snow conditions were a matter of life or death. Before going on a hunt, which could last several days, hunters needed to know if the snow would be the right consistency for building a snowhouse for shelter. That kind of snow was called *igluksaq*, meaning "snow for making an igloo." There are words for fresh powder, snow with wind, and snow that blocks trails. These are a few snow words from a Central Inuit dialect:

▲ The angular face, prominent nose, and dignified bearing of this Cree warrior are distinctly Indian characteristics. He wears a shirt of fringed buckskin and a headdress made of eagle feathers.

aput: snow on the ground
aquilluqqaqa: firm but not quite firm enough for a snow house
ganik: falling snow
masak: wet snow typical of spring
mauya: soft, deep snow
piqtuq: snow being blown in a blizzard
pukak: snow of granular consistency not good for building a snow house

The Inuit also have many words for the different consistencies of mud, which was used, among other things, to make sled runners glide easily through various snow conditions. However, for the dozens of kinds of wildflowers that bloom briefly in summer—pretty but not essential to survival—there is only one word, *nauttiaq*. A missionary in Greenland, in the early 1700s, commented on the complete absence of swear words in the Inuit language.

A VARIED LAND

* * * * * * * * * * * * *

CHANGING CLIMATES

▲ Even in the summer, ice floes are found in the waters
of the Arctic region.

▶ Lichens cover many rocks on the tundra. Slow-growing and very hardy, lichens are an important winter food for caribou.

▼ In the spring along the Arctic coastline, pack ice breaks into chunks, or floes, and drifts in the icy waters.

* * * * * * * * * * * * *

▲ In autumn the tundra in Alaska becomes a vibrant tapestry of wildflowers, grasses, and low-growing bushes and dwarf trees. An old caribou antler can be seen in the foreground of this picture.

THE TAIGA

* * * * * * * * * * * * * *

▶ A typical landscape of the Subarctic region is this bo-real forest of spruce and aspen trees bordered by muskeg, or grassy bog. This autumn scene is in northern British Columbia.

▼ Stately spruce trees dominate this Subarctic forest, characteristic of the woodlands called taiga.

* * * * * * * * * * * * * *

▲ Beauty and grandeur mark this Subarctic scene, now
part of Kluane National Park in Yukon Territory, Canada.

THE TUNDRA

* * * * * * * * * * * * * *

▲ In the summer, purple harebell and red bearberry leaves brighten the tundra landscape in the Talkeetna Mountains northeast of Anchorage, Alaska.

◀ During the brief Arctic summers, the tundra becomes a slushy expanse of vegetation, as in this portion of the Arctic National Wildlife Refuge in Alaska. Rising in the distance are the snow-capped peaks of the Brooks Range.

▼ Alaska stretches past the peaks of the Brooks Range in a vast expanse of snow-covered tundra.

* * * * * * * * * * * * *

▲ A male caribou with a full set of antlers stands on the tundra. Males grow antlers every year for the autumn mating season; they shed the antlers soon after.

CHAPTER TWO

* * * * * * * * * * * * * *

LIVING

The cultures of the Subarctic and Arctic natives were based on a *subsistence* way of life, meaning that they lived entirely off the land. Various groups traded with each other for materials unavailable in their own regions, but their day-to-day survival depended on their success as hunters and fishers, and, to a lesser degree, gatherers.

It is hardly an exaggeration to say that every kind of animal in the Arctic and Subarctic played a role in the lives of the people. Even the larvae of the warble flies that infested the skin of caribou were a treat to Inuit children. They combed eagerly through the summer coats of felled caribou for the sweet, watery larvae, which were eaten on the spot like candy.

Staying alive in the Arctic and much of the Subarctic was a lifelong struggle, which might make one wonder less *how* people survived there than *why* they chose to stay. In answer, the region is far from being a wasteland. The Arctic and Subarctic, as well as the surrounding seas, sustained those prepared to take advantage of the bounty.

HUNTING ON LAND

Caribou, large members of the deer family, once dominated the north of the continent as buffalo did the western plains. Enormous herds numbering hundreds of thousands of animals migrated with the seasons between the Arctic and northerly Subarctic regions. The Inuit living on the Arctic coasts divided their time between hunting sea mammals and caribou. Most Indian groups and the Inuit of the interior organized their lives around the migrations of caribou. Only the Aleut who lived on islands where there were no caribou did not hunt the animal.

The adult caribou averaged about 150 pounds. Its meat was an essential food. Its hide was made into clothing, bedding, tents, canoes, and *babiche*—rawhide strips used for dog harnesses, whips, thongs, rope, and the webbing for snowshoes and fish nets. Caribou bone and antlers were fashioned into numerous implements, such as fish hooks, weapons, sled runners, scraping tools, and sewing needles. Caribou sinew was used for bow string and for thread to sew clothing, tents, and boats made of skin or bark.

The huge caribou herds migrated south in spring to give birth and returned north in July and August. Hunters with spears would wait for them at the mouths of rivers where they crossed; the women stayed on the banks ready to skin the kill. The Inuit devised a more productive hunting method that required the combined efforts of several families. They would set up lines of *cairns*—replicas of humans or frightful creatures made of rocks or sod and sometimes outfitted with antlers and noisy flapping skins. Children and women hiding behind the cairns would scare passing caribou toward the hunters, who were waiting with bows and arrows, or into a lake where hunters with spears waited in skin boats called *kayaks*.

At other times, hunters left their families at camp and traveled great distances seeking caribou. Here, too, the hunt was a cooperative event. The felled caribou were shared by all who joined the hunt, but the man whose arrow made the first successful hit got his choice of meats—the tongue and nose were most often preferred. To

▲ One-person kayaks could be maneuvered with swift precision by skillful sea hunters in pursuit of prey such as seals and otters. A typical kayak was made of seal-skin and was about 16 feet long.

prevent overkill—reducing the animal population by hunting to a dangerously low level—in an area, Indians would agree on "tribal rights" to certain hunting grounds. This helped maintain the ecological balance.

The Montagnais had a custom of leaving meat in trees or on racks at a hunting site so that the next hunters who came there wouldn't go hungry if animals were scarce. Sometimes a portion of the meat would be *cached* (hidden) in snow or permafrost at the site of a kill to be retrieved months later. (Permafrost provided natural refrigeration, which helped to preserve meat for the times of scarcity during the long winters in the Arctic.) The greater portion of the meat, however, was taken back to camp, where the women prepared the feast that followed a successful hunt.

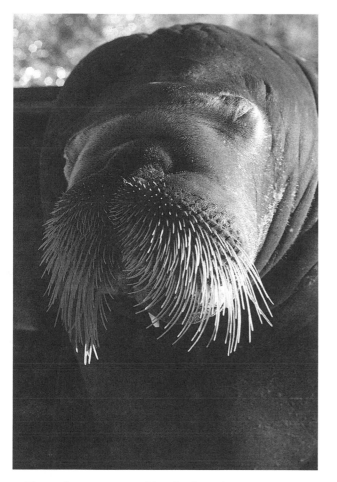

▲ The walrus was prized by the Inuit for its waterproof hide. Walrus skin was used for clothing, tents, and to make skin boats.

The times and directions of caribou migrations were often unpredictable. When the caribou could not be found the people had to hunt other animals. Natives of the Arctic and the most northern Subarctic regions hunted musk oxen. The Netsilik and Copper Inuit, in particular, depended on musk oxen for meat and used animals' heavy, shaggy coats for bedding and tents.

In the densely forested areas of the southern Subarctic, beyond the usual range of the caribou herds, Cree hunters stalked moose. As with caribou, every part of the moose was put to use for food, clothing, tents, and even canoes.

Some Subarctic natives hunted mostly small animals such as hare, squirrel, and porcupine. For small animals, Indian and Inuit hunters used bows and arrows or caught them in traps. The Inuit prized the thick fur of the wolverine for trimming parka hoods because wolverine fur did not trap vaporized air, which otherwise becomes a circle of ice on the clothing around the face. But scavengers such as wolverines and foxes were generally avoided as food, except in extreme scarcity.

For different reasons, bears were not usually the primary object of a hunt. Grizzly and polar bears were too dangerous to hunt, and the liver of the polar bear was poisonous to eat. While bear skins could be used for bedding and tent doors, they were too heavy for clothing. Moreover, the bear was thought to share kinship with humans.

Throughout the Arctic and Subarctic, natives hunted birds such as geese, ducks, ptarmigans, swans, and puffins. In late March, the Cree looked forward to "Goose-Moon," the new moon, which marked the return of migrating geese and the beginning of bird hunting. Cree hunters used short, fire-hardened wooden arrows tipped with serrated bone to shoot the birds.

HUNTING AT SEA

Coastal tribes and the Aleutian islanders built their cultures around hunting sea mammals—walruses, sea otters, sea lions, whales, and especially seals. As with land animals, every part of a sea mammal was put to use. Where trees did not grow, whale bones formed the frame of a house, walrus hides were the walls and roof, and the translucent gut skin of a sea lion or walrus was stretched and dried for a window pane. Seal oil was the primary fuel used to warm homes, cook food, and provide light during the dark Arctic winters.

On the northernmost coast of Alaska, seal hunting began when the sea ice could support a hunter's weight, usually in late October. As the coastal ice advanced into the sea and the weather became colder, the hunters followed, cautiously testing the strength of the ice with long-handled picks and looking for breathing holes. Seals need to surface for air every 10 to 15 minutes, and one seal would have several breathing holes. In the brief moment that a seal appeared, the watchful hunter drove his spear into the animal. Even a successful thrust could end in the frustration of losing the kill to the strong currents surging beneath the ice. Sealing on ice was also dangerous. To prevent slipping and to gain traction on the ice, hunters wore ivory *crampons*

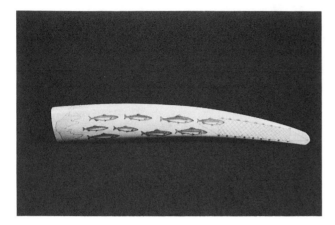

▲ Salmon swim into a fish trap, or weir, in this scene engraved on a walrus tusk by an Inuit.

(studs attached to the bottom of a shoe). If the ice where a hunter stood broke away, he was stranded.

Another risk of hunting came from the blinding glare reflected by the ice. It could cause serious, even permanent, damage to eyes. To solve the problem, the Inuit invented snow goggles, which they made out of wood. Small slits let the wearer see out. Often the goggles were carved to resemble and honor the seals and were objects of beauty as well as function.

The Aleut and many Inuit groups hunted seals and other mammals at sea, a more productive but equally dangerous way of hunting. The hunters rode in kayaks or another type of skin boat called an *umiak*. The kayak is a closed skin boat built for one or two persons (and sometimes for three). The umiak is a larger, open skin boat that carries several people; the larger umiak was necessary for hunting large animals such as walruses, sea lions, and whales. Drownings occurred often. A sudden storm or a surfacing wounded animal could easily capsize or sink a boat in the freezing water.

Aleut and Inuit demonstrated their ingenuity and technical skill in the perfection of their weapons. The toggle harpoon, for instance, was a weapon of such efficient design and craftsmanship that it has been compared to a three-stage rocket. The harpoon head (the toggle) hooked into the prey and twisted so that the animal could not release itself. The toggled head, tethered to sealskin floats, detached itself from the harpoon shaft as the speared animal swam away. In time, the thrashing animal became exhausted and the hunters could easily complete the kill.

▲ Snow goggles are an Inuit invention to protect the eyes from the intense glare of reflected sunlight on ice and snow.

The buoyant skin floats prevented their catch from sinking.

FISHING AND GATHERING

Ocean and inland waters offered fish in abundance and variety, such as salmon, halibut, trout, and shea fish. Fish, however, was not a mainstay for most Subarctic and Arctic natives. Instead, they were a supplement to their diet when caribou migrations changed course or were late, or when caches of meat from spring and summer hunting would not last through fall and winter.

The inland Inuit fished in the tundra ponds for small, oily blackfish to feed their dogs and, when necessary, to relieve their own hunger. Coastal Inuit women, children, and old people sat patiently at holes cut into thick ice, holding braided bark or leather fish lines with baited bone hooks. Inuit men formed teams to pull in fish caught in heavy bark or leather nets (hard work in biting cold water).

Subarctic and Arctic natives were as skillful and inventive in fishing as in hunting, using a

▲ Inuit hunters transport an umiak over land on a sled. These roomy skin boats were used for hunting large prey, such as whales and walruses, as well as for moving households.

variety of methods. Indians dragged Yukon marshes with willow nets and fished rushing streams with long-handled dip nets that currents couldn't sweep away. The Cree set up barricades among reeds growing in muddy river beds, then watched for the movement of the reeds that told them where to wait with their spears for salmon. Ingalik Inuit made baskets in different sizes for trapping various kinds of fish. Aleut kayakers fished for halibut, cod, and herring with baited hooks.

Along the coasts, people set up weirs (dams) at the mouths of rivers to trap char (Arctic salmon). The fish swam upstream when the incoming tide raised the water level above the weir. When the tide went out, the fish were trapped in the weir and then were caught easily.

For most of the year, the Inuit and most of the Subarctic Indians ate meat almost exclusively. In the summer, women and children gathered greens and wild berries. Everyone looked forward to the change in menu.

In times of famine, rock tripe (a gummy lichen) and various kinds of bark, neither one appealing or very nutritious, were gathered and made into soup.

During the spring and summer in the Arctic, people collected the eggs of migratory sea birds. Children and women climbed steep, dangerous cliffs to reach the eggs, each about as big as two chicken eggs. Afterward, the eggs were divided equally among all who joined in the hunt.

TRAVEL AND PORTAGE

The sled was as important to these mobile hunting people as cars are to people today. Subarctic and Arctic natives transported entire households on sleds, following the supply and migrations of wildlife. Hunters who traveled long distances from base camps used sleds to haul home their catch. Whether hand-drawn or pulled by dogs, a sled served best when it was lightweight, strong, and suited to the terrain and purpose.

The typical Inuit sled was 20 to 30 feet long and about a foot high. Its platform was hide or wood, the runners were wood or whalebone, and the crossbars were usually made from caribou antlers. Subarctic groups used a shorter version that handled better in hilly terrain and on steep river banks. Babiche binding (strips of rawhide) held sleds together and gave them the flexibility to handle well on rough trails strewn with chunks of rock-hard snow.

▲ Dog-drawn toboggans are particularly well-suited to the Subarctic terrain, where the Indians needed to move heavy loads over land covered with snow and ice for much of the year.

The sledge was a heavy-duty sled used in the Arctic and Subarctic for moving tents and household equipment, as well as great loads of meat. The toboggan, an Algonquian invention, was designed to glide over light, dry snow. It was a lightweight, flat-bottomed sled that measured from five to eight feet long and turned up in front in a curve that was achieved by steaming the wood.

In the Arctic, and to a lesser extent in the Subarctic, sleds and sledges were pulled by dogs—the only domesticated animal of the Subarctic and Arctic natives. Dogs migrated to North America about 12,000 years ago or earlier, hauling the fur bedding, skin tents, and household gear of their masters. In the Arctic, the importance of dogs was equal to that of horses on the western plains. Without them, winter hunting, fetching cached meat, and trading—survival basics—would not have been possible.

The effort expended to maintain a dog team speaks for its vital importance to the owner. Up to a third of a hunter's time was spent providing food for the dogs, whose diet was mainly seal and whale meat. Dogs on the job were fed only every other day, but each ate as much as a man.

A prosperous hunter might own a team of three to seven dogs, but often ownership was shared. Even one dog had value, for a healthy, adult dog could haul a sled carrying 100 to 150 pounds. As a pack animal it could carry between 20 and 60 pounds.

Inuit dogs, also known as huskies, were fierce. The lead dog of a sled team battled for its position by intimidating or killing the competition. The driver, however, controlled the team. When necessary, the owner waded into a raging dog fight and stopped it, cracking brawlers on the nose with a stick. Reprimands were harsh but were given for reasons that the dogs understood. The owner's purpose was to build an efficient team and to that end disobedient dogs were punished and lazy dogs were killed.

A properly trained team kept a sled moving well, but the driver never rested. He walked or ran beside the sled or sat on top of the load, keeping a constant vigil for seals or caribou, always talking to the dogs, watching their har-

▲ This close-up view of an umiak reveals both the skill of the boatmaker and the courage of the hunters who ventured into freezing and often turbulent Arctic seas to hunt whales in these fragile boats.

nesses to prevent tangles, and checking their feet for ice build-up.

The success of a hunt depended on the good working condition of the dogs. The Inuit customarily fed their dogs before themselves, checked on them periodically through windy nights to make sure they didn't suffocate under snowdrifts, and outfitted them with special boots to protect the dogs' feet from razor-sharp snow crystals.

In addition to hauling and packing, huskies could locate a seal's breathing hole by scent over vast stretches of ice. In some instances, the dogs were companions as well. A hunter might have a parka hood trimmed with the fur of a favorite dog who had died. These dogs were not pets— they were partners in survival. And in times of extreme scarcity, they might be killed for food.

Indians used dogs as pack animals long before they hitched them to sleds, an Inuit innovation. In 1695, a European explorer made no mention of dog teams in his journal but commented that the Cree carried their tents on their backs in summer and dragged them through the snow in winter. In the late 1700s, Samuel Hearne noted that some Chipewyan harnessed dogs to sledges and women pulled the toboggans.

The Indian dog was smaller, thinner, and less hairy than the Inuit husky. A team of eight could pull a toboggan packed with caribou or household goods 20 to 60 miles a day, depending on the weight of the load, the trail conditions, and the dogs' strength. The Subarctic dogs were also used to track small prey and drive moose out of the woods to waiting hunters.

In the Subarctic, a land of lakes and rivers, Indians used canoes for hunting, hauling, and transportation. While the distinctive curve of the bow (the front end of a boat) identified a tribe, certain qualities were standard. Canoes had to be watertight, lightweight for easy portaging (carrying over land), and maneuverable in all water conditions—rough seas, placid lakes, or white-water rapids. The Cree were especially proud of their "crooked canoe," a canoe with a curved bottom. They claimed that it could glide through rapids as well as ride ocean waves.

Canoe frames were formed from saplings or bent wood. They were covered with caribou hides or sheets of birch bark (more durable but not always available) that were stitched together with sinew and sealed at the seams with spruce gum, tar, or pitch. Hunters carried spruce gum and bark with them on trips to repair the damage caused by rocky streams. Mending canoes was a familiar evening activity along the trail.

The Aleut and the Inuit built boats out of skins. Both the kayak and umiak were made of driftwood frames covered with waterproofed walrus gut. The specially treated skin also enhanced the boat's buoyancy.

A long, attentive apprenticeship was required

to learn both how to build a skin boat and how to use one. Maneuvering a kayak in a stormy Arctic sea while chasing a seal or a sea otter, with a spear poised for the throw, took great skill and courage. In umiaks, sailors had to keep their feet carefully positioned so not to disturb the structural balance between frame and skin—a careless moment could be fatal. Of course, any damage, such as a puncture or tear caused by ice or the tusk of a wounded walrus, would have to be repaired immediately at sea, which required special know-how.

Sleds and boats certainly aided mobility, but throughout the Arctic and Subarctic travelers went mostly on foot. Foot gear was survival equipment. Both the Indians and the Inuit wore snowshoes, a Dene invention. They were made of spruce or pine bent into frames with willow or babiche webbing. Two straps held the snowshoe securely to the foot. The shape of a snowshoe revealed tribal identity, and every group had at least two snowshoe designs for different purposes and snow conditions. The Kutchin, for example, made snowshoes up to six feet long for use on fresh snow and a shorter version for packed snow. Northern Ojibway and Tete de Boule were known for diamond-shaped snowshoes with rounded toes; the Swampy Cree snowshoe had rounded toes and pointed backs.

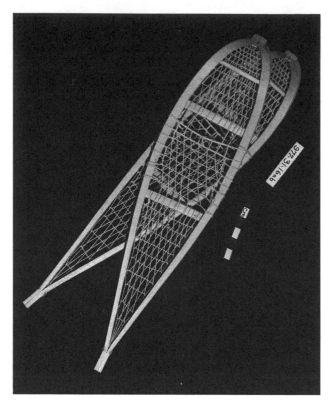

▲ Snowshoes, worn by all the native peoples of the Arctic and Subarctic, were essential for snow travel. By tradition, men fashioned the bent-wood frames, and women prepared the babiche and made the webbing.

THE ROLE OF WOMEN

Matonabbee, Samuel Hearne's Chipewyan friend and guide, blamed the explorer's failure to reach the mouth of the Coppermine River on his first two attempts on his not taking women along. As Matonabbee explained, ". . . when all the men are heavy laden, they can neither hunt nor travel to any considerable distance; and in case they meet with success in hunting, who is to carry the produce of their labor? Women were made for labor; one of them can carry, or haul, as much as two men. They also pitch our tents, make and mend our clothing, keep us warm at night, and in fact, there is no such thing as traveling any considerable distance, or for any length of time, in this country without their assistance. Women, though they do everything, are maintained at a trifling expense; for as they always stand cook, the very licking of their fingers in scarce times, is sufficient for their subsistence."

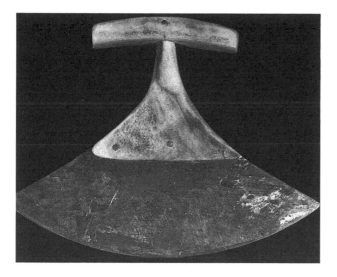

▲ The ulu—the woman's knife—was an all-purpose cutting tool used by Inuit and Dene women.

The Montagnais made wide "bear paw" shoes with tightly woven babiche or sinew netting for deep, powdery snow and cross-country trekking over scrubby, snow-buried trees. Montagnais women also wove patterns such as birds, flowers, and stars into the webbing.

Indians could travel for miles in snow, but John Franklin, an explorer who traveled on snowshoes with some Chipewyan in 1820, wrote that it was a hard walk that "galled the feet and caused the ankles to swell."

MAKING A HOME

In general, among all the Subarctic and Arctic groups, work was divided on the basis of sex. Men hunted and made the weapons, sleds, boats, snowshoes, and tools they used. Every Inuit man had a tool kit containing basic items such as a drill with points of various sizes, an adze (a tool with an arched blade for shaping wood), a saw, and several knives. Two of the most important tools for Indian men were an awl (a piercing tool to make holes in wood) and a crooked knife (used for stripping bark from trees and shaping wood).

Women owned the animals that the hunters brought home. This meant that they skinned and butchered, scraped and chewed (to soften) the hides, sewed the skins into clothing and tents, wove the sinew into webbing for snowshoes, and cooked and preserved the food. Women also helped build shelters. The most important tool

among Inuit and Dene women was an *ulu*—a crescent-shaped woman's knife invented by the Inuit. They used the ulu for scraping hides, cutting and chopping meat, and all the cutting involved in sewing.

In most Indian and Inuit groups, men did the heavier hauling and carrying. Chipewyan women, however, began a life of very hard work at about the age of eight or nine. Women paddled canoes, pulled toboggans, and carried loads often weighing 100 pounds or more.

FOOD AND COOKING

The Inuit and, to a lesser extent, Indians ate their meat raw or just barely cooked. In some instances, raw was preferred, but generally people liked their food cooked and had it that way when possible. For most of the year, the Inuit living along the Arctic coasts had little or no plant life in their diet and saw little sunlight. Even so, they seldom suffered from scurvy, a disease caused by a lack of vitamin C, because raw meat contains vitamin C and other necessary vitamins.

But the real reason for eating the meat uncooked was the scarcity of fuel. In the Subarctic, dry wood could be hard to find, and in the treeless Arctic, driftwood was the only wood. Sufficient moss to make a fire or keep one burning was often unavailable. Supplies of seal oil had to last all winter, and at times, people were forced to choose between using seal oil for fuel or for food.

Boiling was the most common cooking method, but Indians also roasted their meat. Indians boiled food in bark or skin containers by adding hot stones to the liquid. The Inuit boiled meat in stone vessels, which took hours to heat in subzero temperatures and drastically reduced the store of the seal oil—another reason that "cooked" meat was often barely warmed.

Following a successful hunt, women prepared the meat while children kept the dogs and foxes away. Every edible bit of the animal was used. Caribou heads were boiled to make stew; soup was made from blood; all parts of a moose head were served. Leg bones were cracked for the marrow, which was roasted, boiled, or eaten raw. For a beverage, Indians boiled animal scraps to make *sagamite*, a greasy broth.

The heart, liver, and unborn calf of caribou were prized dishes, and the choicest parts went to the men. Montagnais hunters suspected that giving women the select morsels would jinx the

▲ An Indian in British Columbia scrapes the hair from a moosehide being stretched on a frame. Both the man and the boy wear clothing with typical Dene decoration.

next hunt—but in times of famine, a man would give his wife his last piece of food.

When there was meat left over, women cut it into thin strips to cure in the sun, a way of preserving food for up to a year. Fish were cleaned and smoked or sun-dried to be eaten in leaner times. Fish entrails were fed to dogs or cooked down for oil, which was stored in fish bladders and used for cooking. Inuit women whipped berries with bits of caribou fat, seal oil, and snow for "ice cream." Indian women kneaded berries with pulverized dried meat and fat to make *pemmican*, a nutritious food that could be stored for years. Hunters carried pemmican to eat on long treks when prey was scarce.

CLOTHING AND ADORNMENT

Women processed the animal skins, scraping off the fat and chewing the skins to make them supple for clothing. Both the Inuit and the Indians preferred caribou hides for clothing, particularly the mediumweight autumn hides that were free of the holes and scarring caused by insect bites in summer skins. However, any animal skin could be used. The Inuit and the Aleut made

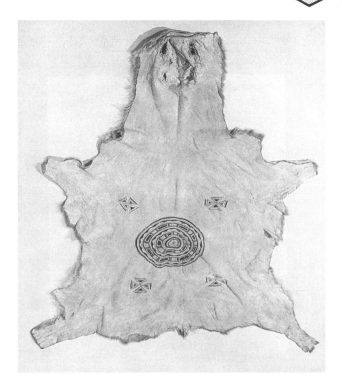

▲ A Naskapi artist painted the geometrical designs on this caribou hide, which was used as a woman's shawl.

▲ This fringed leather pouch, decorated with beads, combines function with beauty and fine craftsmanship. It was made by a Montagnais Indian.

exquisite ceremonial robes from bird skins. Among less prosperous groups, dog skins were sometimes used for clothing. In 1854, the Arctic explorer Elisha Kent Kane reported meeting an Inuit man wearing a fox-fur parka and boots made from the legs of a polar bear, with the soles and claws still attached.

The Inuit who hunted at sea used gut, particularly from the walrus, to make waterproof clothing—parkas, trousers, mittens, and boots—that kept hunters dry as well as more buoyant in the water. (It was not uncommon for a hunter to leap onto the back of a thrashing whale to finish a kill.) For added insulation and comfort, the Inuit wore woven grass socks inside their boots. Inuit-style boots and mittens were adopted by natives throughout the colder regions of the Subarctic.

The parka that many people wear today originated with the Inuit and was readily adopted by the neighboring Chipewyan and Naskapi. The traditional hooded parka was usually made of caribou skin, favored for its light weight and warmth. The parka design conserved body heat by fitting snugly at the neck and wrists and otherwise hanging loose to trap a layer of warm, insulating air.

Sometimes Dene groups are called "people of

the pointed skins" because they wore coats with long pointed tails in front and back. A typical Dene outfit consisted of a long pullover shirt, leggings with attached moccasins, and a breechcloth (an animal skin that hung loosely around the hips and upper legs). The explorer Samuel Hearne noted that a complete winter outfit took eight or more caribou skins.

Cree men and women wore a breechcloth and fringed, tight-fitting leggings, held at the waist by a leather thong and secured below the knee with sinew garters. Men wore long tunics slit at the thighs, while the women's version often had slits under the arms to allow for nursing a child. Detachable sleeves made a tunic an all-weather coat. Many Indian hunters wore beaver or caribou robes secured with thongs across the chest. Such robes could hang loosely for ease of movement or be drawn close for warmth.

All Indians wore moccasins of moose or caribou hide. Even after they adopted some of the European ways of dressing, they rejected hard-soled shoes. Moccasins were quick to make, made no noise, and did not damage canoes or snowshoes. They were comfortable, lightweight, and warm.

Members of every Subarctic and Arctic group

▲ This Cree man reflects both Indian tradition and European influence in his clothing. The woven cloth and beads were probably obtained through trade.

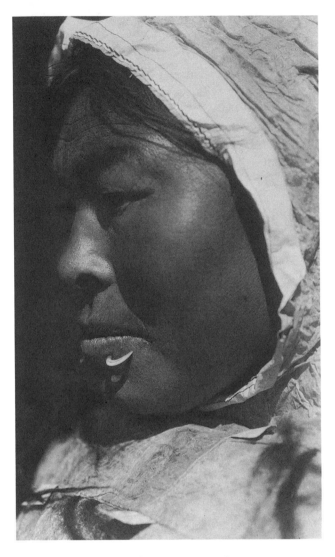

▲ Many Inuit men and women wore lip ornaments, or labrets, inserted in the lower lip (as shown here) or in the cheeks. This hunter is wearing a waterproof parka made of oiled gut skin. Keeping dry while at sea was key to survival in Arctic waters.

had distinctive ways of adorning themselves. Subarctic Indians made extensive use of feathers and porcupine quills to trim clothing. People throughout the Arctic and Subarctic wore pendants and hair ornaments made of teeth, claws, stones, ivory, and bone.

In some tribes, people pierced their noses and ears for pendants or ivory skewers. At the age of 12 or 13, many Inuit boys, as well as girls in some groups, would have a slit made beneath the lower lip at each corner of the mouth in preparation for wearing *labrets*, or lip ornaments.

Tattooing was common among most Arctic and Subarctic groups. Inuit women typically had three blue lines tattooed from the lower lip to the chin; some had more involved patterns on their faces, arms, and legs. Tattoos could symbolize any number of things—marital status, heroism, courage—or just be for looks.

SHELTERS

Subarctic and Arctic homes were either semipermanent or temporary. The feature they all had in common was speed of construction. An Indian family could have a tent up and a fire going in under an hour. In under two hours, an Inuit family could be warming themselves in an igloo while a blizzard raged outside. The Inuit igloo was a strong, warm, dome-shaped structure. Igloos could be made of a combination of driftwood, sod, bark, and skin, or they could be made entirely from snow blocks. However, only the Central Inuit, whose territory had little or no wood, lived in snow houses. For most Inuit, the snow house was only temporary, although it could be life-saving for someone caught in −60° Farenheit winds. For that reason, a snow knife was standard equipment for all Inuit hunters.

The igloo had a tunneled entrance that trapped cold air, helping to keep the living space comfortably warm. Around the inside wall were waist-high sleeping platforms, raised up from the colder air on the floor. Sod igloos had a gutskin skylight, while snow igloos used a sheet of clear ice as a window. When the family moved, they took the ice-window with them because the fresh water needed to make a window was hard to find.

The Aleut and some Inuit groups built pit houses—partially underground structures entered by a ladder through an opening in the domed roof. The frame of driftwood or whalebone was covered by a thick layer of sod blocks.

Every Inuit home had some version of the stone lamp, which was used for cooking, heating, drying, and light. The lamps were usually made of soapstone, a soft, slippery stone. The lamp burned seal blubber using a wick made of moss. It heated the home as it dried clothing. The usual placement of the lamp was under a drying rack

BUILDING AN IGLOO

Although many people associate igloos, or snow houses, with all Inuit, only the Central Inuit people build them. Making an igloo requires skill and practice. Igloos were temporary structures, usually put up to shelter people on a hunting trip.

▲ The blocks for the igloo are cut from the snow using a snow knife. The snow must be right for building. If it is too hard, the snow is difficult to cut and makes a cold house; grainy snow won't stick.

▲ The finished igloo has a passageway leading into it and a small hole in the roof for ventilation. Sometimes the igloo also has a window of clear ice.

where the Inuit hung their clothes immediately after brushing off the snow on entering a house.

A typical Subarctic house was a tepee—a cone-shaped frame constructed out of long poles and covered with bark or skins sewn together. The top was left open for sunlight to enter and for smoke to escape. The floor was covered by pine or spruce boughs and then by a layer of animal skins, usually beaver. In the winter, branches were arranged around the outside of the tepee and packed with snow to keep out cold air. Sometimes several families placed their tepees with the entrances facing toward a communal fire outside.

For temporary shelter, Subarctic Indians would build a lean-to, an open structure covered with bark, branches, or brush and shaped much like a pup tent.

Baskets were an important part of furnishing a home. The focus was always on practicality, but baskets were often works of distinction and beauty as well. The rye-grass basketry of Aleutian women, for example, resembled fine linen. They used strands of rye grass split into threads as fine as silk to make mats, screens, and containers for every purpose.

Other Subarctic and Arctic women made baskets for every need, including wallets, fish sacks, storage jars, and pouches for babies. Typical Inuit baskets were coiled and had lids ornamented with a carved ivory or bone handle. Dogrib women made hunting bags called *muskemoots*, using moose or caribou babiche. The Algonquian invented the *tumpline*—a woven sling that looped around the forehead to support loads hauled on the back.

FAMILY LIFE

People of the Subarctic and Arctic lived in family groups. Living alone was far too impractical and dangerous to be an option in their harsh environment. Parents and children, as well as grandparents, lived together as the primary family unit. As a rule, several families formed a band that traveled and camped together.

Inuit families sometimes formed small, semipermanent villages, rarely numbering over 350 persons and often fewer than 100. Among the Inuit, it was common for two or more families, numbering from 12 to more than 20 people, to share a house. Their living space was cramped. A typical household of 16 people

▲ The nomadic Dene of the Subarctic lived in tepees made of wooden poles covered with skins or tree bark. After contact with Europeans, many Dene began using canvas for their tepees.

cooked, ate, and slept in a shared space that measured no more than 12 by 18 feet.

Generally, Inuit families who lived together were related. All the husbands were responsible for all the wives and children. If one man was killed—a common occurrence among Inuit sea hunters—his wife and children still had a home and a provider. Similarly, Dene and Algonquian families traveled and camped together but tended not to share a tent.

The climate strongly affected the size of the family groups. For example, the Cree, an Algonquian group who faced the yearly threat of winter starvation, were more thinly scattered and on the move than the Ojibway, who lived in a more temperate zone further south. A Cree band typically consisted of no more than three to five families. The Chipewyan, a Dene group, likewise formed hunting groups of several related families. When fish were plentiful or when many

▲ Rectangular tents made of skins were more permanent than tepees, but they were more difficult to construct. Putting up a tent required skill, strength, and speed.

men were needed for a caribou hunt, a community might grow to 600 people.

The Ojibway formed clans (large extended families) that identified themselves by a *totem*— a symbol of a bird, fish, reptile, or other animal that had special meaning for clan members. Like most Indian and Inuit groups of the Subarctic and Arctic, Ojibway clans were patrilineal, meaning that family relationships were traced through the father. Ojibway children, therefore, inherited their totem animal from their fathers.

MARRIAGE

Throughout the Arctic and Subarctic, people married early, at 13 or 14 for a girl and 15 or 16 for a boy. Although customs varied from group to group, certain patterns were widespread. Marriages were often arranged by the parents when the children were very young, sometimes even before birth. Courtship lasted about a year, during which time the young man lived with the family of his prospective wife. If he was a good hunter and got along well with her family, the parents approved of the match and the couple would agree to be husband and wife. With that he would return to his family with his wife. Sometimes a man could take his bride home sooner if he could give her family a year's supply of food in exchange for his work.

Among some Dene groups, "courtship" consisted of a wrestling match; the winner got the wife. It was not uncommon for a man to win and lose the same wife several times in a long and lively evening of sport. The custom of wrestling for a wife was adopted by some of the Inuit whose area bordered Hare territory. But the practice was not common among the Inuit, and the Algonquian Indians scorned it.

In the sparsely populated Arctic and Subarctic, a person might meet only a few hundred people over an entire lifetime, and most of them tended to be relatives, even if they were very distant cousins. It was important to marry—for one's own survival, as well as to perpetuate the tribe— and every tribe had special rules governing the possible choices in marriage partners. For example, among Greenland Inuit, first cousins were considered too closely related to marry. Among the Ojibway, people who shared the same totem were thought too closely related to marry and so they looked for marriage partners outside their clan.

Sometimes there was a great imbalance between the number of marriageable men and women. A very successful Indian or Inuit hunter might have two or more wives. The wives were often sisters. Where men outnumbered women, a woman might have more than one husband, although this was less likely among Indians than the Inuit. Still, monogamy (having only one wife or husband) was the most common arrangement among all Subarctic and Arctic groups.

RAISING CHILDREN

Subarctic and Arctic people felt that childhood should be a time of joy and freedom because adult life was very hard. Children were deeply loved, and their parents rarely spanked or spoke harshly to them. However, childhood was short and officially over at puberty, which, as a rule, coincided with marriage. A typical Greenland Inuit girl, for example, would have no responsibilities other than tending younger children until she married at about 14. Then her life changed abruptly. Her new jobs included butchering animals and preparing their skins for the clothing she would make. She did all the cooking, built and repaired houses, and tended her own children. Relief came only years later when her son brought home his wife to help her.

Mothers cared for their young children, but when a boy was ready—perhaps as early as age eight—he began to go hunting with his father, watching and learning how to be a provider for his own family some day.

SURVIVING

There were sometimes terrible winters in which entire villages—both Indian and Inuit—died of starvation. In the Arctic and the coldest regions of the Subarctic, every member of the family needed to contribute to its survival as early and for as long in life as possible. For that reason, elderly Inuit people sometimes chose suicide when food was scarce and their family faced starvation. Sometimes Indian and Inuit families who had to move camp during winter famine had to leave behind an old person who could not keep up. These were hard, sad occasions, but the emphasis was on life, not death—on the survival of the family, not the individual. Life was a communal, sharing affair in which the greatest sacrifices were offered and accepted for the welfare of the group.

▲ An Inuit mother and her child are dressed in warm furs in this photograph, taken around 1915.

More difficult still was the decision to end the life of a newborn baby. Female infanticide was practiced among Inuit groups when starvation threatened the lives of everyone. In times of extreme famine, a newborn female might be suffocated or placed at the entrance of the igloo to freeze, a decision that was made quickly but only when the alternative was slow and certain starvation. Boys were spared because they were future providers of food and they did not leave the family when they married.

When there was sufficient food for the survival of the whole family, all Inuit children—boys and girls—were cherished.

LIVING ON THE LAND
* * * * * * * * * * * * * * *
ANIMALS OF IMPORTANCE

▲ Caribou, also known as American reindeer, graze on a coastal plain of the Arctic National Wildlife Refuge in Alaska. Vast herds of migrating caribou were once common on the tundra. Today, the caribou must be protected by law.

▶ Grizzly bears fish for salmon at a waterfall on a river in Katmai National Park in Alaska. Salmon, both fresh and dried, was a staple food for many Aleut, Algonquian, Dene, Inuit, and Yuit people.

▼ Dog sleds were used throughout the Arctic and Sub-arctic regions. The Dene hitched their dogs to the sled in pairs so that the team could run easily between trees. In the treeless Arctic, the Inuit hitch their dogs to the sled in a fan shape.

* * * * * * * * * * * * * *

▲ The sea otter was highly valued by many coastal
tribes both for its meat and the warmth of its pelt.

FOOD FROM THE SEA
* * * * * * * * * * * * *

▲ Inuit George Kamookak drops his fish net through a hole cut into the ice at Gjoa Haven on King William Island in Canada's Northwest Territory. Ice fishing is done during the warmer months in the Arctic.

◀ Inuit hunters on St. Lawrence Island, Alaska, butcher a bowhead whale. A village feast of celebration traditionally follows a successful whale hunt.

▼ Fur seals gather on an outcropping of rocks to sun themselves. The seal was a mainstay of the Inuit livelihood, providing food, clothing, and fuel.

* * * * * * * * * * * * *

▲ This beautifully detailed Inuit doll shows all the details of a typical woman's apparel. A baby is nestled on her back; she holds a gathering basket and a large cooking spoon.

EVERYDAY ARTISTRY

* * * * * * * * * * * * *

◀ This detail of an elegant beaded apron in a traditional style is the work of an Ojibway artist from around 1930.

▼ These birch-bark baskets with leather ties combine traditional Dene design with the vivid colors available only in more recent times.

* * * * * * * * * * * * *

▲ This Inuit mask represents the Seal Spirit. The right side of the mask has a model of a seal attached to it.

CHAPTER THREE

RITUAL AND RELIGION

atives of the Arctic and Subarctic shared a view of the world that unified the natural and spiritual worlds. They believed that both humans and animals have souls and that trees, mountains, rivers, wind, ice—all the things that make up the earth—as well as the sun, moon, and stars have spirits. These people strove to harmonize with the forces that governed their lives—the climate, the seasons, and the migrations and life cycles of animals.

Algonquian bands believed in *Manitou*, a mysterious, unseen power that was recognized by the way the seasons change, day follows night, and the sun, stars, and moon move. The Dene and the Inuit looked to their own individual guardian spirits, which often appeared in the form of a bird or an animal. These spirits could help people in times of trouble.

The Inuit referred to the spirits of nonhumans, as well as of inanimate things, as *inua*. The spirit of anything is "its person." They believed the inua of an object could be used to benefit people. For example, the inua of a bear skin was thought to hate death and would therefore drive the sickness out of a sick person who lay on the skin. Another way to benefit from the power of inua was by using things in a respectful and thought-

ful way. Inuit hunters made weapons into objects of beauty and fine craftsmanship, not only to please or attract animals, but also to please the weapon itself and give it life.

The most important relationship, however, for all members of Subarctic and Arctic cultures was between humans and the "animal persons" they depended on for survival. "Hunting is a holy occupation," said a Naskapi, expressing an outlook shared throughout the Arctic and Subarctic. Because animals have souls, it followed that humans survived by eating other souls. Reverence for the animal spirits was central to their religious and daily life, and hunters made conscious gestures of respect so as *not* to offend their prey.

The Naskapi hunted in clothes painted or embroidered with designs they thought would be pleasing to animals. The Central Inuit incorporated ivory carvings of seals into their dog harnesses to honor the seal. Aleut hunters wore their finest parkas when hunting sea otters, who were thought to appreciate well-dressed people. Aleut hunters also wore hats made from wafer-thin pieces of wood bent into shape and decorated with carved ivory, feathers, polished stones, and sea lion whiskers (the number of whiskers signified a hunter's expertise and authority).

All Arctic and Subarctic tribes practiced

"first-fruits" ceremonies after the first animal of a species was taken in a season. A Nunamiut hunter, for example, would hang up the animal's skin for a day and not drink from the family water supply for four days (or five days if the animal were female). He would give his family a careful account of the hunt to ensure continued success. When Chipewyan caught the first fish in a new net, the fish was broiled whole on a fire. Its flesh was removed and the bones burned to bring good fortune to the new net. Hunters of all groups wore amulets (charms) that warded off danger or brought good fortune in every undertaking. A hunter might have the head of tern sewn to his coat to improve his salmon-fishing ability or attach a polar bear's nose to his clothing to give him strength. A fisher might conceal a charm under the bait on a fish hook for luck.

An amulet's power could come from the power of the animal's spirit, or it could come from a *shaman*—a man or woman with spiritual powers. Every Indian hunter carried a medicine bag—a small skin pouch holding sacred items such as otters' teeth, bits of beaver tail, animal claws, and other similar objects meaningful to the hunter. Women were forbidden to touch a

man's medicine bag, for that would take away its power.

Equally as important as charms were songs. Inuit hunters owned secret songs, often passed from father to son, and they would sing their songs going to and returning from a hunt.

OBSERVING TABOOS

Every group had its own *taboos*—rules for avoiding trouble with spiritual forces. Taboos dealt with the unpredictable aspects of nature and reinforced respect for animals. A broken taboo served to explain misfortune, illness, and hunting failures.

Taboos governed all actions related to getting food, from setting up fish weirs to giving slain animals proper treatment. Naskapi hunters, for instance, were careful to keep beaver bones away from dogs so that the beavers would not be insulted and would return in the future. All native groups observed special taboos for placating a bear's soul. When a bear was killed, it was a widespread practice for hunters to eat its heart in a communal meal out of respect for their brotherhood. The Cree would position a bear's skull in

INUIT HUNTING SONGS

This Inuit hunters' song, as told to Knud Rasmussen in 1931, expresses reverence for the animal as well as for the plants the animal eats:

> Great swan, great swan,
> Great caribou bull, great caribou bull,
> The land that lies before me here,
> Let it alone yield abundant meat,
> Be rich in vegetation
> Your moss-food
> You shall forward to and come hither
> And the sole-like plants you eat, you shall look forward to
> Come here, come here
> Your bones you must move out and in,
> To me you must give yourself!

▲ An Inuit woman wears a caribou tunic, mittens, and leggings trimmed with fur from other land animals. A strict taboo prohibited mixing land and sea animals in clothing.

a tree where it could look out over water. Netsilik Inuit performed gestures of respect, believing that the spirit of a bear clung to the tip of a hunter's spear for several days. Unless appeased, its spirit would stay around or return to do harm.

A freshly killed seal, on the other hand, was treated with respect in the hope that it *would* return and give itself again to the same hunter. Believing that sea mammals thirsted for fresh water, women would give newly killed seals a drink. They wanted to give their souls a happy send-off that they would remember. Netsilik wives swept the igloo floor and sprinkled clean snow on it before placing a slain seal on it. Then they began butchering as quickly as possible, scraping the bones clean so as not to offend the seal's spirit with carelessness.

The spirits of caribou, which were thought to be easily disturbed, got special consideration. Women did not scrape caribou skins while a hunt was in progress, nor did they break the bones for marrow until the living caribou had left the area, lest the animals see their own kind suffer at the hands of humans. Indians in the Great Slave Lake region of the Northwest Territories once blamed a famine on a hunter who had chased a caribou through the snow to exhaustion, beating it with a stick.

Strict taboos dealt with the conflict believed to exist between sea and land animals. Meat from sea mammals was cooked over a blubber lamp, not over caribou oil. Caribou and seal were never cooked in the same pot or served together at the same meal, and hunters did not eat seal meat on a day they hunted caribou. Women did not work on caribou hides during sealing or on sea mammal hides during a caribou hunt, and the skins of sea and land animals were never combined in the same garment.

At all times, thoughtful action preserved the fragile human-animal relationship. Indians told stories about animals only in wintertime when they slept so not to rouse their indignation at being talked about. Alaska Inuit hunters refrained from boasting about their hunting conquests, and they concealed negative emotions from animals. Before a whale hunt, they observed rites of purification—cleaning their equipment, having new clothes made, making a new cover for their boat, and sleeping apart from their wives. At the moment of the kill, the hunter apologized to the animal. Young Inuit boys were taught to "make way for the seals" by keeping the animals they would

one day hunt foremost in their minds. Inuit girls were trained to sew skillfully, for sloppy stitching offended an animal's spirit and could spoil the hunt.

In some Inuit groups, women helped their husbands while they hunted by remaining inactive, imitating the way they hoped the animals would behave. Even though women's thoughts and actions were considered vitally important to the hunters' success, they were always in second place. No Inuit or Indian woman would step over a man's legs as he stretched out before a fire, and men avoided a woman's gaze. Around hunters, Inuit women kept their eyes downcast and Dene girls shielded their eyes with a basket or hood. Eye contact with a woman was considered a frivolous and dangerous waste of a hunter's valuable eyesight.

Taboos and rituals concerning womanhood and birth were carefully observed because they had to do with perpetuating the tribe. Special rites marked the occasion of a girl's first menstruation. She might be isolated for several days to several months. In some tribes she spent that time in a special hut. Throughout their childbearing years women would perform rituals of purification following menstrual periods. A mother could improve the prospects for health and a happy future by keeping an unborn child in her thoughts at all times and carefully observing taboos.

THE SPIRIT WORLD

Native people of the Arctic and Subarctic lived in fearful respect of wandering animal ghosts and human souls (who could be either helpful or destructive) and numerous supernatural forces. The unseen spirits influenced all the important elements and events in the natural world—most importantly the weather and the food supply.

The shaman was the vital link between the human world and the realm of spirits. A shaman, sometimes called a medicine man or medicine woman, was the most powerful member of the band. Shamans had two major responsibilities: preventing and healing sickness, and interpreting messages from the spirit world.

▶ Shamans, like this Alaska Indian medicine man, were the link between the people and the spirit world. People both revered and feared shamans for their power to control evil spirits.

RIPPOWAM CISQUA SCHOOL LIBRARY
Rippowam Campus, Box 488, Bedford, N.Y. 10506

A shaman, who was usually a man, got his power from spirits who appeared to him in a dream. A young person who wanted to become a shaman would go into isolation and fast to prepare for a vision—a trancelike experience.

Illness was thought to be caused by an evil spirit entering a person's body or by the person's soul leaving. In northern Alaska, it was believed, for example, that wandering souls of children could get caught on thorny berry bushes. Signs of soul-loss were discouragement and listlessness. A shaman was called on to retrieve an errant soul or drive a harmful spirit from a body where it did not belong.

An Indian medicine man forced evil out with sweatbaths or "sucked" it out, sometimes spewing out a mouthful of claws, shells, and stones afterward. His payment was made on the spot, for patients feared the cure could be reversed. It was not unusual for a shaman to be wealthier than others.

Only Inuit shamans could "fly," or send their spirits great distances while in a trancelike state. An *angakok*—an Inuit shaman—could "fly to the moon" (meaning to make fertile) to get a baby for a childless couple. He could also call on Narssuk, the weather spirit who lived in the sky and loathed humankind. Narssuk stirred up blizzards by loosening the thongs that held on his caribou skins. If an angakok succeeded in tightening the thongs, the weather calmed. A shaman could locate caribou herds through spiritual travel to Nuliajuk, the sea deity, to find out why hunting was poor. He could send a *turnaq*—a shaman's own protective spirit—or go himself to retrieve a precious but easily lost tool, such as an ice chisel, harpoon, or iron needle.

The shaman helped people cope with the great mysteries and suffering in their lives. Why famine? Why sickness? In some Inuit groups, people gathered in a tent where the angakok trembled and fell into a trance, conversing with spirits in a secret language to learn why the people were suffering. Typically, a general taboo was named, such as the separation of sea and land animals, and people who had violated that taboo would begin admitting their wrongdoing. Group confession was an important part of the spiritual life among the Central Inuit.

◀ This ceremonial Inuit mask was made in the Kuskokwin region of Alaska near the Bering Sea. It is made of carved driftwood ornamented with feathers and pigment.

An angakok gained people's confidence by surviving tests, such as being "burned alive" or by being "thrown into the sea under ice with hands and feet tied and stomach pierced with a spear." The test continued out of view of the audience, and when the shaman returned unharmed—neither burned nor wet nor bound—people did not probe to find out how the feat was performed.

Shamans in Subarctic tribes performed "tent-shaking" ceremonies to prove they were genuine. Indians gathered outside a special tent with no door. Inside, the shaman, bound tightly with cords, kneeled. As spirits entered the tent, it began to shake more and more violently. Voices of different birds and animals could be heard as their spirits imparted information for tribe members that only the shaman could interpret. Afterward, the shaman would appear, exhausted and wet and mysteriously untied.

While shamans brought benefits to their people, they also caused worry. Their power came from spiritual forces and was as likely to be evil as good. They could turn their power against people. A dead shaman was not necessarily a safe one because his soul could stay around and cause harm.

People of the Subarctic and Arctic believed that the spirit world was populated by beings who could either behave in the best interest of humankind or stir up trouble. At the start of a trip, Chipewyan would always make a gesture of appeasement to the spirit of the wind for calm weather. If setting out in a canoe, the traveler might scatter tobacco on the water or offer the smoke from a pipe to pacify the spirits of rivers, rapids, and rocks.

Netsilik Inuit feared dreadful ghostly beings, giants, and dwarfs with human qualities, who always disappeared from sight, but whose fresh tracks were seen in the snow. There was the fiery Ignersujet who never slept, and the big-bellied, humanlike Narjet, who could catch a caribou on the run and eat it all. Women who too often played string games such as cat's cradle—a favorite winter pastime—had to watch out for attack by Totanguarsuk, the dangerous spirit of string figures.

Inuit hunters would see half-man, half-monster creatures that glided along without legs and could hypnotize a person to death. In the winter, shamans were called on to protect people from being devoured by such demonic spirits.

Dene feared the Bush Indian, a half-man, half-animal creature who attacked lone hunters and ate their fat. Algonquian lived in terror of *windigos*, monsters who devoured people and spit them out again as cannibals. A Cree version was *matci manitu*, flame-breathing spirits that flew through the dark, hunting victims.

Stories of dreadful, people-eating monsters helped people to cope with the grim reality that cannibalism occasionally occurred when people were crazed by hunger. European explorers sometimes painted a picture of Indians and Inuit as cannibals for their enthralled listeners back home, but the truth is that *all* native people looked on cannibalism with horror. The unfortunate person driven to it lived with the disgust and fear of fellow tribe members ever after. The "windigo disease" was considered incurable and the afflicted person was likely to go insane.

THE SOUL'S JOURNEY

The native people throughout the Arctic and Subarctic believed that the soul lived on after physical death. Ideas about the afterlife varied in some details from group to group, but, in general, people believed that the soul stayed near its body for a period of time following death—anywhere from three days to a few years—and that it was important to free a soul to make its journey to another world or back to this one.

A widespread belief among the Inuit was that a soul passed through many animal lives before

HUNTERS AND PREY

The hunter's relationship to his prey was a combination of violence and reverence. Many stories dealt with those opposite emotions by depicting humans and animals in various relationships, from being spiritual kinfolk to ancient enemies. The following tale, written down around 1865, is an example of a story that resolves the conflict created by having to kill beings who are not enemies:

OUR ANCESTORS

The daughter of the moon spirit was the bird wife of the first man on earth. Their children were the ptarmigan and the grouse in many nests all over the tundra. As time went on, these birds dropped their wing and tail feathers and walked the earth as human beings. They were our first ancestors.

The trees standing in clumps, the flocks of wild geese we see in the autumn, the herds of caribou whose paths we cross in the snow, the wolf packs hounding them—who are they? All, all people like ourselves not so long ago. Yet sometimes they appear to their human brothers in dreams, and harass them.

Long, long ago, the ways of life were still uncertain. People and animals resembled each other and changed at will. Birds one season, they were people the next and game the following year. For who are the caribou if not our former enemies of the Beaver tribes in disguise? They were punished by the spirit of death for our benefit, that we may feed upon them. So do the wise ones still tell us in the winter nights.

▲ Music and poetry—often sung or chanted to the accompaniment of at least one drum—were an important part of Inuit culture.

resuming human existence. Many Inuit also believed that the spirit of the recently deceased could be reborn as the next child in the family. Hence, it was not unusual for an Inuit child to be called "Grandfather" or "Auntie" by his or her older relatives.

Burial customs in the Arctic and Subarctic combined people's spiritual beliefs with practicality. Long winters everywhere and permafrost in the Arctic made underground burial extremely difficult. Bodies were therefore "buried" above ground, sometimes in a box, sometimes laid on a pile of driftwood, and sometimes on a burial platform. Often stones or driftwood were heaped on the body or it was encircled with rocks to lessen exposure to animals.

Various Inuit and Indian groups dressed their dead in new clothing and left offerings of food, clothing, and tools at the "grave" for the soul's use long after death. Chipewyan, on the other hand, wrapped the body in skins and left it on the ground to be eaten by scavengers—the reason that wolverines, foxes, and ravens were avoided as food, except in severe famine.

The rebirth of a soul into a new body in this world was considered good; hanging around the living in spirit form was not. All Subarctic and Arctic groups observed death taboos before and after "burial" in order to urge a soul to move on. Ignoring such taboos could enrage a spirit, which might then stay around and become an annoying or even deadly pest. Some Inuit groups removed

▲ The blanket toss, now a popular game at Inuit festivals, was originally done to boost a hunter up to sight sea mammals at a distance.

a corpse from an igloo through a window, the smoke hole, or a specially made opening to befuddle the soul and prevent it from finding the way back. "Doors for the dead" were common among Algonquian tribes as well, and sometimes an Indian camp moved immediately following the funeral rites.

The Cree, who would occasionally see lingering souls in the rolling fogs over marshes, would bury a weapon with its owner so that the ghost would not return to search for it or haunt the camp. Some Inuit would sweep the igloo where the dead person had slept in life and then crowd the space with objects to force the soul out, or place a knife at the entrance of an igloo, sharp edge outward, to turn a returning soul away.

The Cree believed that once freed from earthly bonds, the soul came to a river that it crossed with ease if in life the person had been unselfish and lawful. The spirits of troublemakers, however, were transported by murky waters to a cold wasteland and endless suffering. The Baffin Island Inuit believed the souls of those who had been kind and never killed in anger lived on in a place where there was no ice, snow, or storms.

For the souls of lazy hunters and women who lacked the courage to have tattoos, however, there was a dreary underworld realm. There, hungry spirits huddled with their heads drooping—their only food being butterflies that flew close enough to be caught. The Inuit placed as much importance on how one died as on how one lived. Punishment did not follow a death caused by childbirth, suicide, or an accident while hunting.

Several Inuit groups shared some ideas about the soul that were unique to Inuit culture. They believed that a person had three souls—the immortal spirit, which lives on; the "lifetime-soul" or breath, which ends at death; and the "name-soul," which lives in the person's name.

After death, the name-soul waited at the burial site until called by the next child born in the family. The child given the *atka* (or name-soul) also gained the deceased person's wisdom

▲ Whale stomachs were dried and stretched on frames to make the drums used by this Inuit dance orchestra. This photo was taken at Point Barrow, Alaska, in 1935.

and skill. Parents were not to scold a child too much because doing so could offend the atka, which in turn could harm the child with sickness or even death. An atka became the child's guardian spirit, for a newborn's own soul was like the baby, weak and apt to be foolish. Having a name-soul had other benefits, too. At the annual Feast for the Dead, held by Alaska natives, souls of the departed were honored and their namesakes were given gifts of clothing and food.

CELEBRATIONS

Celebrations among the Arctic and Subarctic natives were a rich mixture of spiritual renewal and the love of a good time. The Naskapi built large winter tents especially for dancing. The Cree would construct a roomy brush enclosure with a huge fire in center and hold a great ceremonial feast. For as many days as the food lasted, people danced and ate their fill.

Alaska natives lived where reliable food supplies allowed them to turn their attention to a round of winter festivals. Hunters held contests in archery and club-throwing. Children played blanket-toss and ball games with animal bladders, which they inflated or stuffed with grass. Four colorful events that brightened the long, dark winter were the Bladder Festival, the Feast of the Dead, *Petugtaq* (a gift-giving festival), and the Messenger Feast.

The Bladder Festival celebrated the rebirth and renewal of life. All year long people saved the bladders of the sea mammals they killed. (It was thought that an animal's soul was located in its bladder.) Just before the festival, the bladders were inflated, painted, and hung about the *karigi* (the ceremonial igloo) as the honored guests. Men purified their bodies with sweatbaths and their homes with smoke from wild celery stalks. After a great deal of celebration and feasting, the bladders were gathered and returned to the sea to reunite with their souls. People hoped that the bladders would tell other animals to give themselves to the hunters who had treated them well at the festival.

TRADITIONAL DANCE DRUMS

A modern Inuit musician wearing a traditional skin parka proudly displays his drum, measuring about two feet in diameter. Inuit drums are shallow and open, resembling tambourines. Drumheads are made of caribou skin, whale liver or stomach, or walrus stomach stretched over a wooden frame. Some drums have handles made of bone, wood, antler, or ivory.

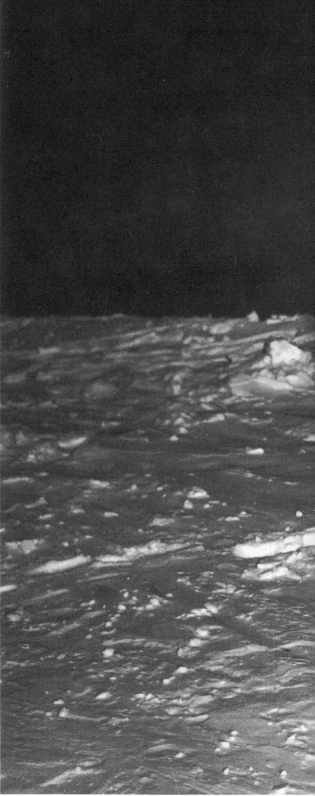

▲ Among the Inuit, dancing is inseparable from singing, chanting, and drumming.

The Feast of the Dead honored the souls of deceased friends and relatives, and freed them from earth. Celebrants lighted lamps and sang songs of invitation to guide the souls to the karigi. There, people performed dances that imitated walking on snowshoes or paddling a kayak to encourage the souls to move on. Everyone received gifts of food, utensils, and clothing, with the most valuable gifts going to the namesakes of the souls being honored.

For Petugtaq, another gift-giving festival, men would hang miniature replicas of things they wanted—grass socks, birdskin caps, skin mitts—on sticks. The women wove and sewed these things, not knowing for whom. "Odd couples" made by pairing the maker of the gift with the receiver created some moments of great hilarity.

The Messenger Feast was a ritual for exchanging goods between villages. The feast got its name from the custom of sending a messenger from one village to another with an invitation. The messenger carried sticks bearing pictures of gifts the hosts desired, and people made up songs to describe the gifts and to please the animals whose bodies provided the materials.

Music and dancing were always part of celebrations in the Subarctic and Arctic. Chipewyan used a circular hardwood and caribou skin drum—two quick raps and a pause—to accompany chanting and circle dances. The Cree used flat round drums of bent willow hoops and deer skin that hung from one hand by a thong. The Inuit wore masks and danced to an orchestra of bladder tambourines, clattering animal teeth, and rattles of snail shells or clanging hoops.

Every Indian and Inuit tribe had its own versions of the drum dance. For instance, the Cree drum dance re-enacted the trickery of Wisaket-cak, a creator and trickster, and mimicked the movements and calls of birds. (In one story, Wisaketcak had beguiled flocks of birds into a bag and was busily wringing their necks when the cautious loon opened an eye, saw the calamity, and flew off to warn the others.) In the traditional Inuit drum dance, the men stripped completely and the women stripped to the waist as the dance gained momentum. Native peoples delighted in their folklore and took nakedness in stride.

STORIES AND THE SPIRIT WORLD

The ancient stories of the Subarctic and Arctic natives, like the stories of other early cultures, helped people make sense of their world. How did the world begin? Where did humans and animals come from? How did the sun, moon, and stars come to be? Why is there suffering?

The Labrador Inuit told about Tornga'rsoak, a father so embittered by losing his children that he sent misfortune into the world. Thunder and lightning, many Inuit believed, were caused by

HOW WARMTH CAME TO THE WORLD: A DENE STORY

Once, long before people lived near the Great Slave Lake, the winter came and never ended. All the animals of the forest got together to discuss the problem—except for the bears, who at that time lived in the upper world above the sky. As the animals talked about how cold and hungry they were, a wise old fox suggested that perhaps the bears knew why the winter was lasting so long. All the animals decided to go search for the bears. They found a hole in the sky and went through it into the upper world. There, by a beautiful lake, they found a huge bear guarding a heap of leather sacks. The animals hid in the woods and watched. Soon they saw that inside one sack was rain; in another, snow; in another, wind. Inside the largest sack was warmth.

The animals decided to steal the sack holding warmth. The caribou lured the bear off into the woods while the other animals took the sack. The bear quickly realized he had been fooled. He gave up chasing the caribou and began chasing the other animals, but they had a big head start. Just as the bear caught up to them, the animals jumped through the hole in the sky and landed back on earth. They opened the sack and let the warmth out to end the long winter.

two girls shaking skins and striking a flint in fury at their ill-tempered father. The Cree envisioned a Thunderbird winging across the sky, raising a deafening racket and shooting lightning from his eyes. Answers to many questions were given in stories like those, handed from one generation to the next. They entertained, they explained, and they gave meaning to the activities and experiences of everyday life.

Some Dene groups, as well as the Inuit from Alaska to the Mackenzie region in Canada, explained their origins with stories about Great Raven, who created the world and gave it culture. A story from the Bering Strait region explains that Raven dropped beach peas on the bare earth and from each pea sprang a full-grown man. Raven then shaped clay into pairs of animals and finally a woman for the first man, and the peopling of the world followed. Another story tells how, through trickery, Raven became the grandchild of an Inuit whaling captain. As the child, he asked for light as a toy in the form a ball. Then Raven broke the ball to give everyone light. His mother wanted the light divided into a larger and smaller light so that people could have darkness for resting at night. Raven granted her wish, and made the sun and moon. Raven was creator, provider, and trickster.

Wisaketcak (the comical character who inspired the traditional Cree drum dance) remade the earth from a handful of mud after a flood destroyed it. The Hare, Chipewyan, and Dogrib tribes traced their origins to a dog and more trickery. One version of the story tells of a woman who married a dog who appeared to her in the shape of man. She discovered the deception and in despair, she destroyed three of her six pups. The survivors—a female and two males—transformed into humans and began the Dogrib tribe.

The most important deity among Arctic peoples was the Sea Goddess, called Nuliajuk in the west and Sedna in the east. She was the mother of all sea mammals and the enforcer of taboos. One version of the Sedna story tells about a beautiful girl who married a man-animal—first a dog and then a temperamental sea bird. Her father attempted to rescue her in his kayak, but a bird followed and stirred up a storm. Her father then cast Sedna back into the sea, but she clung to the boat. Unable to pry her loose, her father chopped off her fingers. The fingers were transformed into all the sea mammals, and Sedna became their ruler.

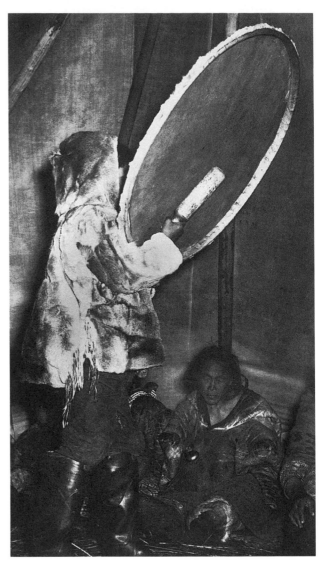

▲ An Inuit dance usually started with a few beats tapped on a drum. The pace would get faster as more and more people joined in as dancers or drummers. A skilled drummer was a valued member of an Inuit community.

Sedna always knew when someone violated a taboo. She could make a seal vanish from under a harpoon and frequently did, having no great love for humankind. But when appeased, she could be a generous provider of animals.

From time to time, a shaman would journey to Sedna's sea home to "comb the vermin of broken taboos" from her hair. Since Sedna had no fingers and could not do this herself, the combing calmed her anger. The Netsilik ritual of group confession was a way of "combing Sedna's hair," for when all violations of taboos had been admitted Sedna released animals to be hunted.

CELEBRATING A
STRONG CULTURE

* * * * * * * * * * * * * *

DENE TRADITIONS

▲ Dogrib drummers accompany themselves in song.
Their flat, round drums resemble those used by Inuit and
Cree musicians.

▲ These ancient rock paintings, or pictographs, were
made by ancestors of the Dene hundreds of years ago.

▲ A modern Dene woman gathers herbs for medicine.
Notice the beautiful beadwork on her mittens and the
artistic detail on her jacket and leather pouch.

CEREMONIAL MASKS

* * * * * * * * * * * * *

▲ A Labrador Inuit made this dance mask from sealskin. Since Inuit men do not have much facial hair, this mask may be a parody of a white man.

▲ Carved from wood and adorned with feathers and pigment, this Inuit ceremonial mask shows the careful work of the artist.

▲ Inuit dancers improvised mostly on survival themes such as hunting, picking berries, or gathering eggs. No subject was too trivial to imitate in dance.

INUIT TRADITIONS

* * * * * * * * * * * * * *

◀ Modern Inuit dancers perform for visitors at Kotzebue on the western Arctic coast of Alaska. Gloves are always worn, no matter what else an Inuit dancer does or does not wear.

▼ Members of a touring Baffinland Inuit theater group share their culture and art with the outside world.

* * * * * * * * * * * * * *

▲ Inuit Sally Karatak models a traditional beaded dress outside the Prince of Wales Northern Heritage Center in Canada's Northwest Territory.

CHANGE

uropean explorers were drawn to
the strange and austere land of the
Arctic and Subarctic by the
excitement of adventure, by the
hope of finding an all-water trade
route from Europe to Asia, and by
the potential for riches—especially
in whaling and the fur trade. They
brought significant changes to the people of the
region. European manufactured goods such as
blankets and firearms found eager acceptance.
The contact, however, also brought devastating
problems.

Most Native Americans had their first encounters with Europeans in the period between about
1400 and the late 1800s. Historians call this time
the contact period. The first contact between Europeans and the Inuit, however, actually occurred centuries before this period. Thorfinn
Karlsefni, a Scandinavian adventurer, may have
been the first European to bargain in the New
World for furs when he encountered Greenland
Inuit (whom he called *skraelings*) in 1004. Ac-
cording to legend, Karlsefni exchanged cow's
milk for a bundle of valuable pelts.

THE HUNT FOR THE NORTHWEST PASSAGE

Later, "the hairy men from the east" (so named by
an Algonquian chief) crossed the Atlantic Ocean
in search of an all-water route to Asia. Instead of
finding the legendary Northwest Passage, they
discovered a rugged new land full of wonders.
And among the wonders were the remarkable
peoples of the Arctic and Subarctic regions of
North America.

In 1576, Martin Frobisher, an English explorer, set sail for India from the Shetland Islands, off the northern coast of Scotland. His
westward voyage brought him instead to a bay
off Baffin Island (now named Frobisher Bay),
where he spotted several wary Inuit in skin
boats. Frobisher captured an Inuit man, kayak
and all, and returned with him to England where
the "strange man and his bote [sic] . . . was such a
wonder onto the whole city and to the rest of the
realm. . . ."

Two hundred years later, no water route to
China had been found. However, Alexander
Mackenzie, an adventurous Scottish agent for the

▲ Inuit hunters harpoon a whale at Point Barrow, Alaska, in 1935. The abundance of whales and valuable fur-bearing animals brought commercial hunting and terrible destruction by Europeans to the Arctic.

North West Company (a fur-trading company), thought a river flowing west from Hudson Bay would take him to the Pacific Ocean. His 1796 expedition led him to a great river, now called Mackenzie River, which flows north along the Mackenzie Mountains through the Mackenzie Territory into Mackenzie Bay. (Explorers were tireless in giving their own names to Indian landmarks.) He apparently did not meet the Mackenzie Inuit, but he made several contacts with Indians that helped expand the fur trade.

In the early 1800s, for three summers, the waters surrounding Greenland became unusually clear of ice. New hope arose for a way to China through Arctic waters. British sponsors of the Ross Expedition in 1818 reasoned that continued exploration would pay off, despite past failures to reach Asia. The search for the Northwest Passage, after all, had resulted in the mapping of the New World and led to rich sources of furs and whales.

WHALING

As early as 1590 European whale boats by the hundreds were venturing into the pack ice of the Arctic seas. Whale oil was in high demand for use in lamps and for other purposes, as was *baleen*—the flexible, hornlike material found in a whale's upper jaw. The Inuit used baleen for bows, combs, and other tools; Europeans used it, among other things, for the stays in corsets that made waists fashionably slim. The oil and baleen

from just two whales paid for all the expenses of a whaling expedition and made a profit.

For the most part, the Inuit welcomed whalers, feeling that the sea and its bounty belonged to everyone. On occasion, Inuit men worked on whaling ships as crewmen. Moreover, whalers brought goods that were of great value to the Inuit—mosquito netting, violins, sunglasses, and most especially guns. Some Inuit learned new dances, such as the American square dance and the Scottish reel. Seeing the sailors play football on the ice, the Inuit created their own version of the sport using a sealskin ball.

However, the relationship between the Inuit and the whaling crews was not always friendly. Violent encounters were usually over food shortages and Inuit women. The whalers also introduced alcohol to the Inuit—the "strong water" that did them great injury and led to violence and even murders. The other deadly import was foreign disease, such as measles, smallpox, tuberculosis, and influenza, against which the Inuit had no immunity. In 1899, sailors from the *Active*, a whaling ship that stopped at Southampton Island, brought sickness to the Sadlimiut group, which left all but five dead. By 1900, the entire Inuit population was reduced by two-thirds from

what it was estimated to be at initial contact, due to epidemics and the starvation that followed when the stricken people were too weak to hunt.

Wherever the whale ships went, the animals disappeared. After baleen whales were hunted to near extinction, whaling crews hunted walruses for ivory and seals for fur. They killed musk oxen, bears, and foxes just for their skins, and captured hawks to sell to falconers.

By 1915, commercial whaling was essentially over in the Arctic. Plastic had replaced baleen, petroleum had replaced whale oil, and whales had become rare. The surviving Inuit faced extreme hardship and famine. They owned rifles that could make hunting easier but had lost their source of ammunition. Even in the "good old days" of 1817, the Inuit had paid a high price for European goods: a hand-carved wooden eyeshade purchased only one bullet.

THE FUR TRADE

For most adventurers, the great attraction of the Arctic and Subarctic regions was fur. In 1534, a French explorer, Jacques Cartier, sailed up the St. Lawrence River hoping to find a way to China. When he was stopped by impassable rapids near present-day Montreal, he met Indians eager to trade furs for knives and beads. Cartier returned to France laden with furs. This was the almost accidental beginning of the extensive fur trade that spread across North America, building fortunes for white investors and subjugating the native suppliers.

Inspired by Cartier's good fortune, in 1603 Samuel de Champlain, another French explorer, sought new sources of furs. He ventured far into the northern woods, making trade agreements with various tribes to supply pelts to French trading posts.

In 1610, Henry Hudson, an Englishman navigating a Dutch ship, sailed into James Bay. There a lone Cree man approached the ship, eager to exchange pelts for a knife, a mirror, a hatchet, and a few buttons. The stage was set for the fierce competition that followed between opportunists organized into two rival companies, the Hudson's Bay Company and the Compagnie du Nord (Company of the North). Each fought for control over the fur trade with the Indians.

The Hudson's Bay Company was begun in 1670 by two Frenchmen, Pierre-Esprit Radisson and Medard Chouart Groseilliers. These two ambitious fortune-seekers persuaded King Charles II of England to grant them a charter giving the Hudson's Bay Company control over

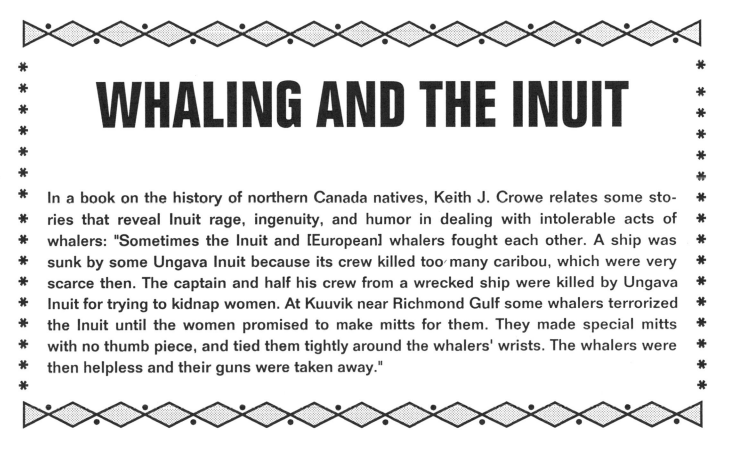

WHALING AND THE INUIT

In a book on the history of northern Canada natives, Keith J. Crowe relates some stories that reveal Inuit rage, ingenuity, and humor in dealing with intolerable acts of whalers: "Sometimes the Inuit and [European] whalers fought each other. A ship was sunk by some Ungava Inuit because its crew killed too many caribou, which were very scarce then. The captain and half his crew from a wrecked ship were killed by Ungava Inuit for trying to kidnap women. At Kuuvik near Richmond Gulf some whalers terrorized the Inuit until the women promised to make mitts for them. They made special mitts with no thumb piece, and tied them tightly around the whalers' wrists. The whalers were then helpless and their guns were taken away."

all the resources included in 1.5 million square miles, "all the rivers and lands to be discovered" from Hudson Strait to the Pacific Ocean. The area encompassed most of what is now Canada.

Beaver fur was then the rage in European fashion, and North America seemed to have an endless source. The king was assured that furs would bring unimagined profits, and the idea that the land and its resources belonged to the Indians never came up.

In 1679, the French established the Compagnie du Nord (Company of the North) to compete with the very successful Hudson's Bay Company for the fur trade. The Compagnie du Nord was made up of independent traders and *voyageurs* (professional woodsmen) who scouted out sources of furs and Indian trappers to supply them. They set up posts from Labrador to the interior of Canada, where the Hudson's Bay Company had not yet ventured. At that time, the Hudson's Bay Company had trade centers only on the coast and Indians had to travel great distances to do business with them.

Algonquian trappers were shrewd in business, and they realized that competition between the French and English companies could be used to boost the value of pelts. Their good business sense, however, was often destroyed by alcohol, an aspect of the competition that did the Indians great harm. The rival companies offered liquor to attract native business, using the alcohol to set the mood for bargaining, to celebrate a deal, and to pay for skins. Too often, native trappers exchanged many valuable pelts for a paltry amount of cheap whisky. Alcoholism, a tragic legacy from the fur-trade days, continues to destroy the lives of many Subarctic and Arctic natives.

To the northeast, on the west coast of Greenland, Lutheran missionaries entered into the fur trade in the 1720s. German Moravian missionar-

THE FUR TRADERS

Beginning in the early 1600s, the Europeans' demand for furs brought white traders to the Native Americans of the Subarctic. The traders offered the Indians manufactured goods such as cloth and metal implements in exchange for pelts. The arrangement was very profitable for the traders. For many of the Indians, however, the arrangement led to over-hunting and cultural destruction.

The Hudson's Bay Company, founded in 1670 and still active today, is the oldest and most famous of the fur-trading companies. A rival firm, the North West Company, was founded in 1783 and was taken over by the Hudson's Bay Company in 1821. The careful reproduction of a North West Company trading post shown here is now part of Grand Portage National Monument on the western shore of Lake Superior in Minnesota.

ies entered the fur trade in 1771, setting up combined trading posts and missions on the coast of Labrador. The chief interest of the missionaries, however, was to take religion to the "heathens" in the "uncivilized" parts of the world—to win souls, not amass fortunes. Their trading posts supported the missions and missionary families; the competition between the groups was for converts.

Unlike the commercial trading posts, where liquor could be purchased with pelts, the Moravians bartered only with practical goods—guns, ammunition, clothing, and building materials. They wanted to provide Inuit and Indian trappers with a market where they could get European goods along with European religion.

In 1741, while the French and English were vying for dominance in the fur trade in the eastern and central Subarctic, the Danish explorer Vitus Bering, sailing under the Russian flag, explored the Aleutian Islands off the coast of Alaska. He learned that the Aleutian waters were a rich source of fur-bearing mammals and that the Aleut were excellent hunters. The sea otter pelts that members of Bering's crew took back to Russia brought the *promyshlenniki* (Russian fur traders) looking for more. These traders used guns to force the native hunters into service. They held women and children hostage until the men produced enough seal and otter pelts. If hunters failed to meet the "quotas," their families were killed.

In 1761, the Aleut organized against the Russian trade ships. For five years they attacked foreign boats with deadly fury until an entire Russian fleet crushed their resistance. Russian traders ravaged not only those who served them but their means of livelihood as well. Steller's sea cow, a large, peaceful sea mammal that once flourished in the Aleutian waters, was hunted to extinction within 25 years after its discovery by the traders. In another 20 years, sea otters, too, grew scarce and the traders moved on to unexploited areas, leaving ruin behind.

In exchange for a fortune in furs, the promyshlenniki brought the Aleut destruction—violence, alcohol, and disease. The effect on the Aleut population and culture was devastating. In the mid-1700s, they numbered about 20,000; by the end of the 18th century approximately 2,000 Aleut survived, impoverished and defeated.

At the same time, in Canada, the Compagnie du Nord and the Hudson's Bay Company were pushing westward. Also at that time, in Europe, the French and English were engaged in a war that ended French rule in Canada in 1763. The Compagnie du Nord was dissolved, leaving the French canoe routes in western Canada unclaimed—but not for long. Free traders, not associated with the Hudson's Bay Company, took over abandoned routes and continued moving farther into Dene country in a contest with each other for Indian trade.

Competition from the Compagnie du Nord, and the subsequent rivalry from independent traders, caused the very confident Hudson's Bay Company to rethink its tactics and begin exploring areas inland for setting up trading posts. In 1769 Samuel Hearne, an adventurous agent for the Hudson's Bay Company, was chosen to explore "far to the north, to promote an extension of our [the English] trade, as well as for the discovery of a North West Passage. . . ."

On his three expeditions in the years between 1769 and 1772, Hearne walked nearly 5,000 miles, covering an area stretching from Churchill on Hudson Bay to the mouth of the Coppermine River at Coronation Gulf on the Arctic coast. Along the way he kept an informative and colorful journal, formed a lifelong friendship with his Chipewyan guide Matonabbee, and concluded that a northwest passage through Hudson Bay did not exist.

During those same years, following the withdrawal of the Compagnie du Nord, the independent traders, the "Nor'westers," began to see that fighting among themselves hurt their business. Therefore, they joined forces and formed the North West Company in 1779. The Hudson's Bay Company countered the threat of the newly organized competition by setting up posts along the same trade routes. The battle lines were drawn; even worse, the tribes took sides.

Natives formed alliances with competing profiteers, who often set them against each other or played on their ancient rivalries. Cree territory encompassed the Hudson's Bay Company posts, and the Cree vigorously protected their own involvement in the fur trade from the intrusion of Chipewyan and other tribes. Getting into the spirit of foreign business practices, they would purchase a gun at the trading post for 14 skins and sell it to neighboring tribes for 36.

With ready access to guns, the Cree had little trouble overtaking Chipewyan trade. They made raids along the Mackenzie River and turned their

former allies to the south, the Blackfoot and Sioux tribes, into enemies. In time, Cree lands were overhunted and overtrapped, and the Cree themselves were reduced in number by the spread of European diseases. When Cree power declined, surrounding Dene tribes stood ready to fill the void, and similarly, the Chipewyan had their day. Following the Chipewyan were the Yellowknife who dominated Slave, Dogrib, and Hare hunting grounds for 30 years, until the Dogrib fought back. Scarlet fever, however, did more to undermine the Yellowknife reign than the Dogrib did. The Lac de la Mort, or "Lake of Death," was so named because scarlet fever erased a Yellowknife band who camped nearby.

For over 40 years, the Hudson's Bay Company and the North West Company clashed with ferocious intensity, but the match was uneven. The Hudson's Bay Company had a tighter and more disciplined organization, as well as English sea power, giving the "Company" the advantage in delivering the European goods. In 1821, the Hudson's Bay Company absorbed the North West Company, and the competition for controlling the fur trade ended. By then, the trading posts had other trappers, as well as Indians, to supply furs. The Company no longer needed Indians quite as much as the Indians needed the goods gotten in trade, especially flour, matches, guns, and ammunition.

The Hudson's Bay Company continued moving west, further into the Mackenzie region.

Along the way more Inuit became involved as trappers, guides, interpreters, and diplomats, who smoothed hostilities between various Indian and Inuit groups. However, the Inuit had not yet entered into the fur trade on a significant scale. Two things happened to bring them into the fur trade—the collapse of whaling in 1915 and then the rising price of Arctic fox pelts, popular during the 1920s.

During those years, the Hudson's Bay Company set up posts throughout the northern regions of Canada and for 10 years, until the fur industry foundered in 1930, a few Inuit made a great deal of money. A fox pelt could be sold for between $30 and $70.

As they had earlier when the whalers left, the Inuit faced ruin when fur prices collapsed. The wildlife, hunted for fur and food, was depleted. The trading posts themselves had altered the caribou migrations. By the 1920s, the traditional way of life was over for all but the most remote Inuit of central Canada.

GOLD RUSH

Many non-natives who ventured into the Subarctic and Arctic regions did not join in the fur trade, but they still viewed the land as a potential source of wealth. In 1870, a prospector combing the Northwest for gold met an Alaska Indian who gave him two gold nuggets. Word spread and gold seekers poured into the Yukon.

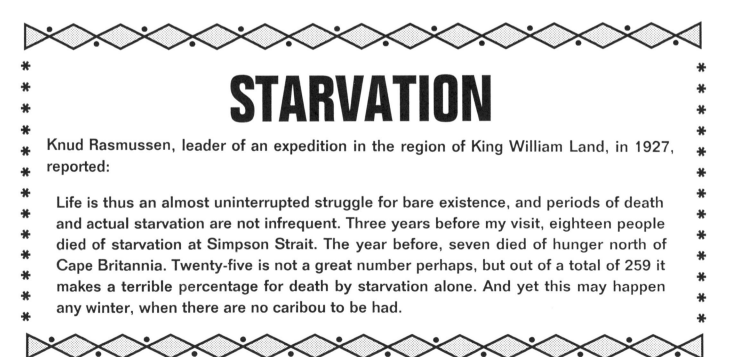

STARVATION

Knud Rasmussen, leader of an expedition in the region of King William Land, in 1927, reported:

Life is thus an almost uninterrupted struggle for bare existence, and periods of death and actual starvation are not infrequent. Three years before my visit, eighteen people died of starvation at Simpson Strait. The year before, seven died of hunger north of Cape Britannia. Twenty-five is not a great number perhaps, but out of a total of 259 it makes a terrible percentage for death by starvation alone. And yet this may happen any winter, when there are no caribou to be had.

▲ Furs could purchase such useful items as the canvas used to make this Inuit family's summer tent and the metal file that the man has made into a snow knife. Before European traders brought metal to the Inuit, snow knives were made of bone or ivory.

The gold rush was a boom time for some Indians while it lasted. They could make $100 a day packing heavy mining equipment over the mountains. Of course, the cost to them was also high when the contact-destruction pattern repeated itself. The stampede for gold ravaged the land and wildlife and brought the natives liquor, disease, and racial prejudice. Even as late as the 1940s, signs in the windows of some businesses in Alaskan towns read: NO NATIVES SERVED HERE and NATIVES NEED NOT APPLY.

CHANGING LIFEWAYS

Before contact, native people were exposed to only a few types of disease and were generally

very healthy. After contact, they struggled for survival against epidemics of whooping cough, measles, smallpox, and scarlet fever, among other contagious illnesses. Tuberculosis was unknown among Alaska natives before 1770, but by 1814 it was rampant. In 1780, smallpox wiped out 90 percent of the Caribou Chipewyan. In 1928, the last of the surviving Yellowknife died in a flu epidemic.

The traditional lifeways of all native peoples of the Subarctic and Arctic were based on subsistence—living entirely from materials supplied in nature. The fur trade moved the native peoples toward a money economy, meaning that they needed money to buy many things they needed and wanted. Put in another way, native people shifted from complete independence, or self-sufficiency, to dependency on outsiders to supply essentials. Guns and ammunition, imported from Europe, became necessities, especially as animals grew scarce. Because there were fewer animals, other materials had to be imported and bought to make clothing and tents and for food. Tobacco and tea also came from the outside and had quickly become necessary luxuries.

Trading for goods was not new. Native groups had long exchanged materials through trade agreements or gift-giving festivals. But trading in furs was different. Animal skins were "spent" like money. For example, a *made-beaver* (a top-quality pelt from a mature beaver) was worth a fixed amount. Two top-quality otter skins or 10 pounds of goose feathers might equal the value of one made-beaver. Therefore, a pound of thread that cost a made-beaver also could be bought for two otter skins or 10 pounds of goose feathers.

The switch to using money instead of furs was not a great leap. In fact, the first coins minted to make trading easier bore the image of a made-beaver. A coin's worth was signified by how much of a made-beaver was stamped on the money. For example, a coin showing one-quarter of a made-beaver was worth one-quarter of a made-beaver in trade. The coins could be spent like money in Hudson's Bay Company stores.

Among the many items that traders offered in return for skins were the means to get more skins—an advantage to both the trappers and the traders. Moravian missionaries introduced seal nets, which made seal hunting easier. Instead of standing motionless for hours at one breathing hole, waiting for a seal to surface, a hunter could set nets around several at a time. Seals would become entangled in the nets. European traders in-

troduced steel traps, which enabled hunters to cover huge areas with long trap lines. The traps increased the fur harvest but were extremely cruel to the animals.

The gun, which arrived in the mid-1600s with the early explorers and traders, made the biggest difference in hunting. Muskets, the first firearms, had several obvious drawbacks. They were heavy, awkward, and none too accurate. They could take as much time to use as a bow and arrow and were apt to blow up, claiming a hand or a life in the explosion. But they brought prestige and authority to the owner, intimidated human enemies, killed from a distance of 100 yards, and increased the yield of pelts. When repeating rifles were introduced in the 1860s, the gun quickly became the hunters' basic tool of survival. The gun transformed their lives and land.

For people who had looked on starvation as an inevitable part of life, the rifle seemed a marvelous gift. It required far less skill than a bow and arrow. Now a hunter didn't have to chase a caribou until he himself was exhausted. A seal hunter could camouflage himself behind a white, hand-carried shield and crawl over the ice to within shooting range of unsuspecting seals. In

▲ Cree Indians traded furs for canvas and other fabric as well as for blankets, saddles, and hats. Like many other Native Americans, they adopted and modified those European things that enhanced their traditional lifeways and ignored those that did not. These Cree continue to wear comfortable moccasins.

the excitement of owning a rifle, hunters, who had previously used every particle of an animal, sometimes killed a caribou just for its choicest parts and left the rest to rot or for scavengers to eat.

Non-natives, however, led the slaughter, often hunting solely for sport—an activity quite alien to native people. Food supplies diminished. One explorer of northern Canada in the early 1800s reported seeing between three and four million caribou; in 1967, the Canadian Wildlife Service estimated that the total caribou population in Subarctic and Arctic Canada was under 200,000.

Caribou fell to disease, predatory animals, and habitat destruction, but the grand thinning was due mostly to overhunting. Natives had lived for centuries in ecological balance with the animals on which they depended. Their occasional bursts

of "rifle madness" had little to do with the sweeping disappearance of wildlife. Non-native greed, ignorance, and expansion, on the other hand, had a great deal to do with it.

The mass-kill tools that replaced the traditional native weapons also undermined the relationship between humans and nature that had been central to native spiritual life. Reflecting on the large-scale exploitation, Smohalla, who led a hunting–gathering band along the Columbia River, said ". . . the work of the white man hardens the soul. . . ."

RELIGION AND EDUCATION

Lutheran missionaries first arrived in 1721 in Greenland with the purpose shared by all missionaries—to "civilize" and Christianize the natives. As the fur trade spread westward, other Christian denominations followed, usually establishing their missions near trading posts, or as in the case of the Moravians, setting up their own trade centers.

Missionaries quickly saw a need for schools in order to teach their religions. For that reason, various missionary groups translated religious texts into native languages, thereby preserving a vital part of native culture that would have otherwise been lost. In Greenland missionaries established the first Inuit school in 1740 and taught reading and writing in the Inuit language. Jesuit, Episcopalian, and Russian Orthodox missionaries also taught scripture in native languages.

In addition to spreading their religions, missionaries helped natives in material ways. The Moravians encouraged the Inuit to produce and sell artwork to help them survive in a money economy. Among some southern Subarctic tribes, missionaries introduced farming to head off starvation—a well-intended idea that did not catch on among hunters and gatherers who were always on the move. Many missionaries brought medical help in an effort to stop the horror of raging epidemics, but most of all they brought their own religions and rules.

While the trading companies competed for the

ECOLOGICAL DESTRUCTION

Between 1826 and 1838, John James Audubon, an American artist and ornithologist, traveled in Canada as far north as Labrador, studying and painting birds. He also observed with sadness the damage that had been done to the Indians, writing in his journal:

> . . . the aborigines themselves [are] melting away before the encroachments of the white man, who looks without pity upon the decrease of the devoted Indian, from whom he rifles home, food, clothing, and life. For as the Deer, the Caribou, and all other game is killed for the dollar which its skin brings in, the Indian must search in vain over the devastated country for that on which he is accustomed to feed, till, worn out by sorrow, despair, and want, he either goes far from his early haunts to others, which in time will be similarly invaded, or he lies on the rocky seashore and dies. We are often told rum kills the Indian; I think not; it is oftener the want of food, the loss of hope as he loses sight of all that was once abundant, before the white man intruded on his land and killed off the wild quadrupeds [animals] and birds with which he has fed and clothed himself since his creation.

▲ European missionaries brought their religious beliefs to the people of the Arctic and Subarctic. This Russian Orthodox shrine stands on Native American land in Alaska.

natives' business, the agents of peace and morality fought each other for their souls. Sometimes efforts to recruit native converts led to hostility between family members and groups who chose different sects. "Civilizing the heathens" did more to extinguish Indian and Inuit cultures than the hundreds of years of exploitation by fur traders and fortune seekers had. The missionaries came not to claim riches but to change the people.

Change began with the suppression of all aspects of native culture judged unholy—native dances, songs, rituals, and various festivals. Missionaries routinely gave native people new (usually European) names, a very personal assault on their heritage.

The attitude that native people had everything to learn and nothing to offer guided the education policies of both mission and government schools in Greenland, Canada, and Alaska for decades. For a long time, educators believed that native people needed to be assimilated—absorbed into the dominant, non-native culture. In essence, assimilation meant giving up being an Indian, or an Inuit, or an Aleut and becoming a "non-native." The key to assimilation was for everyone to speak the same language.

From the early 1900s through the 1960s, Inuit children in Greenland learned Danish; in Canada, French or English; in Alaska, only English. Even mission schools that had previously used texts in native languages began to teach only in one non-native language. Children were punished for speaking their native language in school, and their parents were advised that they could best help their children by not using their native language at home.

In the 1960s, in Canada and the United States, attitudes changed and native languages were re-instituted in school curriculums. The Bilingual Education Act of 1967 in the United States requires schools to offer instruction in native languages. Sadly, several Inuit and Indian languages had disappeared by 1970 when the last people who spoke them died. Dr. Michael Krauss, the leading Alaska native linguist, has predicted that by 2055, most of Alaska native languages will be extinct and that the Dene language will be spoken in only a few scattered settlements.

Another aspect of educating natives was taking students from their villages and putting them in boarding schools for their secondary education. There, they learned the "right language" as well as "civilized ways." For instance, Inuit children raised on seal and caribou meat were taught that a "balanced diet" included fruits such as oranges—exotic fare in the Arctic. At school they ate with knives and forks, slept between sheets, and lived in plain but warm rooms. Young people returned home unable to communicate with their parents, ashamed of their old world, but not ready for the new one. Graduates who had not learned traditional survival skills could not live on the land, but they also couldn't get jobs off the land. Even when they had the skills for modern jobs, prejudice against native people kept them from being hired.

Consequently, many young people dropped out of school early, discouraged and wondering where they belonged. By the 1980s, alcoholism had become the primary epidemic sweeping native populations. In Alaska and Canada, the suicide rate for Indians and Inuit is four to six times higher than national averages. The greater number of suicides is no longer the elderly who feel unproductive, but young men who see no future.

LAND CESSIONS AND TREATIES

Two events in the late 1700s promoted British expansion into Canada: New France, the French colony, came to an end, and England lost the revolutionary war in the United States. The new English-speaking settlers brought with them an old idea: the Indians should agree to cede (give up) their rights to the land. Many treaties (agreements) of that kind were made, starting in 1817. In all, the treaties offered Indians little in return for a lot—nearly all the southern half of Canada. The details of individual treaties varied little. Generally, in exchange for surrendering their rights to their land, the Indians got reserves (called reservations in the United States); a small one-time cash payment to the tribe; ammunition; clothing, medals, and flags for the chiefs; the promises of continued hunting and fishing rights; and annuities—yearly payments made thereafter to each band member (usually about $5 per person).

While negotiating terms, government officials made verbal comments that the Indians took as promises. For example, when Chief Pierre Squirrel signed over Cree, Beaver, Chipewyan, and Slave lands to Canada in Treaty Number 8, in 1899, he believed that the government would provide doctors. Later, he recalled bitterly that when a measles epidemic struck in 1903, his

8

tribe got "nothing but missionaries."

The *written* promise that Indians valued most—the "right to sell or hunt, trap, and fish in the ceded area"—had no meaning after hunting grounds were buried under modern cities.

A happy tradition, however, that began with the treaties was the celebration of Treaty Day, when the Indians received their annual payments. On Treaty Day, Indians would hold festivals for feasting, dancing, sports, gambling, and trade. In the early years, government officials came in person to hand the money to band members. Now the yearly payments are sent by mail, but Treaty Day celebrations have continued in Canada.

In 1867, Russia and the United States negotiated a treaty in which Russia transferred its sovereignty over the Alaska territory to the United States for $7.2 million (approximately two cents an acre). At the time, the Inuit were scarcely aware it happened, and other Alaska natives were prohibited from watching the signing ceremony. Part of the treaty, however,

guaranteed protection to the "uncivilized tribes" and, most importantly, recognition of their land rights.

The United States Congress did little to back up that guarantee, as a succession of non-natives intruded into native lands—gold seekers, commercial salmon fishers, whalers and trappers, and the military. But when oil was discovered in 1968 on the North Slope (the region of north Alaska between the Brooks Range and the Arctic Ocean), the Inuit were drawn into the active protest that had been gaining momentum since the formation of the Alaska Native Brotherhood, organized by southeastern Alaska natives in 1912.

RESISTANCE AND ASSERTION

Resistance to non-native takeover was less violent and certainly less organized in the northern territories (now Canada) than in the country to the south (now the United States). The primary

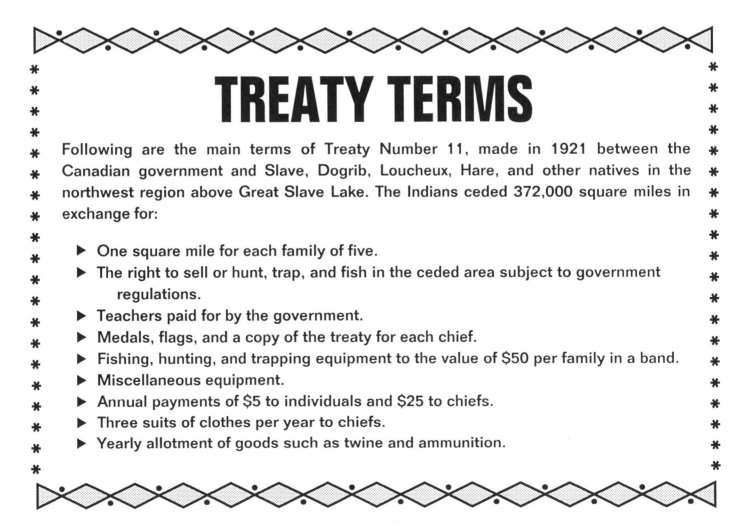

TREATY TERMS

Following are the main terms of Treaty Number 11, made in 1921 between the Canadian government and Slave, Dogrib, Loucheux, Hare, and other natives in the northwest region above Great Slave Lake. The Indians ceded 372,000 square miles in exchange for:

▶ One square mile for each family of five.
▶ The right to sell or hunt, trap, and fish in the ceded area subject to government regulations.
▶ Teachers paid for by the government.
▶ Medals, flags, and a copy of the treaty for each chief.
▶ Fishing, hunting, and trapping equipment to the value of $50 per family in a band.
▶ Miscellaneous equipment.
▶ Annual payments of $5 to individuals and $25 to chiefs.
▶ Three suits of clothes per year to chiefs.
▶ Yearly allotment of goods such as twine and ammunition.

▲ A section of the Standard Oil Company's pipeline stretches north of the Yukon River. When this photograph was taken in 1978, there was a revegetation program underway to restore the natural ground cover.

enemies in the Arctic and Subarctic were cold and famine, which kept the population low and left native peoples little time to wage war against each other or newcomers. The distribution of food supplies caused people to live in small, scattered bands, making an organized defense against invasion difficult.

The French, who first penetrated the Subarctic region, wanted furs, not land. The fur trade did not crowd people off their land as the British farmers did later. Moreover, the French cultivated the goodwill of the Indians, who they needed as guides and trappers. Many French woodsmen learned Indian languages and adopted their lifeways. Intermarriage between Indians and the French further promoted peaceful coexistence and resulted in another distinct group, the Métis—people of French and Indian heritage.

Nevertheless, the native peoples of Canada have not fared better, over all, than those in the United States. The percentage of native people now living in poverty, alienated from their old world and lost in the new one, is about the same in both countries. What they have lost is cruelly clear to them, and they are now organizing to use non-native systems—law and politics—to fight back and force their governments to honor treaties.

As soon as oil was found in 1968 on the North Slope of Alaska, oil companies set up rigs and derricks and began making plans for a pipeline to carry the oil across Alaska to waiting tankers, which would then carry it to refineries. The construction of the pipeline was an enormous undertaking that would tear up the land and bring in an entire community of workers and businesses.

The rush for oil threatened to have the same devastating effects on the land and wildlife that earlier greed for fur and gold had had. The Inuit organized. Their leaders pointed out to the United States government a serious flaw in the scheme: There could be no permit to build a pipeline until old, unresolved claims to native land rights had been settled. The Inuit stance

was that Russia's sale of Alaska to the United States in 1867 was invalid because the land belonged not to Russia but to the Alaska natives. An Inuit leader, Charlie Edwardsen, Jr., argued their case before Congress, saying, "If the United States is prepared to buy the Arctic Slope or to rent it, the Eskimo are prepared to negotiate, to discuss terms." Etok (Edwardsen's Inuit name) knew he could not stop the flow of oil; he fought instead for the Inuit's rightful share of the profits.

The fight resulted in the Alaska Native Land Claims Settlement Act (ANLCSA) of 1971—the largest settlement in the history of Native Americans. Alaska natives were awarded ownership of 44 million acres of land and compensation totaling $962.5 million for giving up title to 330 million acres of land. ANLCSA stipulated that title to land rights would be divided among several native corporations made up of individual shareholders. At the time of the signing the *Tundra Times*, an Inuit newspaper, called ANLCSA "the beginning of a great era of Native people of Alaska."

In the years following the passage of ANLCSA, some serious problems have developed. A major disappointment to Alaska natives has been that most of the money gained has had to be spent in putting ANLCSA into effect. Also, Alaska natives are divided on the issue of having individual shareholders, meaning the ownership of land by individuals. The traditional Indian and Inuit way has always been shared, or communal, ownership.

In 1971, the government of Quebec began a massive project to produce hydroelectric power for Quebec, as well as for sale to the United States at immense profits. The plan calls for di-

verting and damming all the major rivers of northern Quebec that flow into James Bay—an area of 140,000 square miles. Creating huge dams to control the water will flood and erode the land, drown some rivers out of existence, and reduce others to trickling streams. The hydroelectric project means destruction of the hunting grounds of the Cree and Inuit living in the James Bay region. Creating such radical changes in the natural environment upsets ecosystems and endangers all plant and animal life. The Cree protested the hydroelectric project in court and got an order that put a temporary stop to the project. Then, in 1975, the Cree and Inuit of the James Bay region signed a land claims agreement with the Canadian and Quebec governments. In return for surrendering their claim to the land, they got $225 million, ownership of lands around their villages, and exclusive rights to hunt, fish, and trap over a greater area.

The James Bay agreement was the first of its kind to be settled in Canada after the Office of Native Claims was established in 1974 to review and act on claims over land rights and treaty obligations. The first big "win," however, involved great loss and got mixed reactions.

In his book *Strangers Devour the Land*, Boyce Richard quotes Cree hunter Job Bearskin's immediate response to the James Bay and Northern Quebec agreement: "There will never be enough money to pay for the damage that has been done. I'd rather think about the land and think about the children. What will they have when that land is destroyed? The money means nothing." Bearskin expressed a view commonly shared by native peoples about legal battles that end in cash for land.

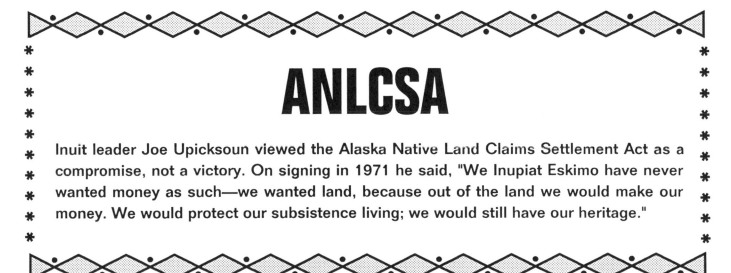

ANLCSA

Inuit leader Joe Upicksoun viewed the Alaska Native Land Claims Settlement Act as a compromise, not a victory. On signing in 1971 he said, "We Inupiat Eskimo have never wanted money as such—we wanted land, because out of the land we would make our money. We would protect our subsistence living; we would still have our heritage."

▲ Three modern Inuit women, wearing traditional parkas very similar to those worn by their ancestors hundreds of years ago, stand next to an airplane, now as important to many Arctic villagers as sleds once were.

▲ Grand Portage National Monument in Minnesota is near the Ojibway Grand Portage Indian Reservation. Many Ojibway today sell their traditional craftwork to visitors.

THE TRIBAL MOVEMENT

The term *tribal movement* refers to the actions that Native Americans are taking to keep their cultures alive. Alaska, Canada, and Greenland natives regard their struggles to survive culturally as Dene, Algonquian, Aleut, and Inuit as one great movement. Three primary motivations guide the tribal movement: to protect native land rights and lifeways; to solve social problems that create poverty and destroy lives; and to revive and perpetuate the cultural heritage of native peoples—their languages, arts, music, stories, and rituals.

Historically, the objective of non-native governments has been to protect and assimilate native peoples. Put another way, governments treat natives as "children" and try to blot out their cultural uniqueness. The tribal movement rejects "parenting" and assimilation, opting instead for self-determination and cultural identity. Natives argue that they must have their ancestral lands in order to continue their traditional lifeways. About 70 percent of the Alaska and Canada natives now live in settlements remote from cities—in small villages in Alaska and on reserves in Canada. Their livelihoods combine subsistence with a money economy (dollars come largely from government assistance, sales of native arts and crafts, and wages). Money buys equipment such as snowmobiles, outboard motors, chainsaws, fuel, and rifles, which are used for subsistence activities. Native people who live and work in cities sometimes return to their villages and reserves during hunting seasons to participate in traditional subsistence lifeways.

Poverty, however, remains a fact of life for a great many native people, whether they live in rural communities or in cities. While the reasons are many, alcoholism has been both a leading cause and result of poverty and related tragedies, from broken families to suicides. Several tribal governments in Alaska and Canada have stopped allowing alcohol to be brought into their communities. As a result, some groups who had been caught up in alcohol abuse have redirected their energies to rebuilding their homes and their lives.

The aspect of the tribal movement most visible to non-natives, however, is the renewal of native arts that are shared with the world. The Institute of Alaska Native Arts sponsors festivals, exhibits, and workshops to promote the visual and performing arts. Alaska native children can attend culture camps where they learn their tribal languages, stories, customs, arts, and rituals. Artists combine traditional and new ideas in sculpture, painting, drama, literature, dance, and music.

LOOKING AHEAD

The survival of the native cultures of Alaska, Canada, and Greenland is not assured. Competition for land and resources between natives and non-natives still threatens traditional lifeways. Poverty and racism continue to be destructive and potent enemies. But there are some encouraging developments. The tribal movement to maintain a culturally rich heritage is strong and vital, giving the present new meaning and native peoples new hope for the future. The Inuit, Aleut, Dene, and Algonquian are growing in strength and unity. They have shown remarkable skill in the use of powerful non-native weapons—law and politics. The Inuit in Canada are working on plans for an Inuit province, "Nunavut," meaning "Our Home." Nunavut would be created from portions of Canada's Northwest Territories, and in 1982 the proposal won government approval. Talks are currently stalled while exact boundaries are determined and Dene–Métis land claims on bordering areas are resolved. The population of Nunavut would be largely Inuit, giving them the space and political leverage needed to carry on their lives as they wish.

▲ This child, dressed in traditional skin clothing, may become one of the first citizens on Nunavut, a proposed Canadian province that would belong to the Inuit.

In 1987, at Point Borrow, Alaska, Inuit leaders from Alaska, Canada, and Greenland gathered for the first Inuit Circumpolar Conference. They debated and made resolutions concerning their land claims, wildlife rights, and cultural survival. Intense discussion focused on how land should be used. The delegates passed a resolution that points the way to Inuit survival in the future and reflects how they have used land in the past: The Arctic should be "used exclusively for peaceful and environmentally safe purposes." It's an ancient idea whose time has come for the survival of the whole earth and *all* its people.

MODERN LIFE

* * * * * * * * * * * * * * * *

TRIBAL CULTURE TODAY

▲ A modern Inuit family poses for the camera. Most Inuit
today preserve traditional elements in their clothing but
also use modern fabrics.

▲ At the annual Inuit Arctic Games, an athlete demon-strates the high kick.

◀ Old and new lifeways exist side by side for many Alaska Natives. Here salmon dry on a traditional frame in front of a modern wooden house.

▼ The modern architecture of the Cree tribal headquarters in Canada reflects the spirit of a people who accept their new role as a positive political force in a world that threatens their cultural heritage.

* * * * * * * * * * * * *

MODERN ARTISTS

* * * * * * * * * * * * *

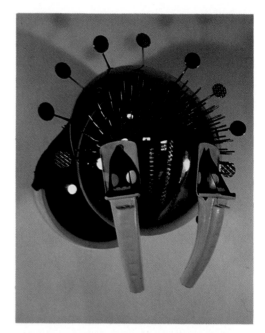

▶ This modern sculpture by Inuit Larry Beck uses modern automotive materials—chrome hub caps, rubber tire, and reflectors—to honor the animal spirit of the walrus.

▼ Modern Inuit sculpture is avidly sought by collectors all over the world. This humorous carving by artist Judas Dotoolah is made of soapstone and ivory.

* * * * * * * * * * * * *

▲ Monica and Ida Kapakatoak proudly display their modern tapestry depicting a very traditional theme—ice fishing.

DAILY LIVING

* * * * * * * * * * * * * * *

▶ A stop sign in both English and Inuit stands guard against reckless driving in a modern Arctic village. Snowmobiles are the most common vehicles here. Because the ground is always frozen beneath the surface in the Arctic, telephone poles have to be mounted in huge tubs of concrete.

▼ A Métis worker on an oil rig in northern Canada smiles through the cold. The Métis are descendants of French trappers who came to Canada in the late 1700s and married Cree women.

* * * * * * * * * * * * * *

INDEX

PICTURE CREDITS

Alaska Division of Tourism: 58, 70, 91 top; American Petroleum Institute: 85; Atlatl: 92 top; Brooklyn Museum: 35 left and right, 54; Channel Islands National Park: 45 bottom; Alissa Crandall: 42 top, 43, 71 top; Edmonton Air Museum/Northwest Territories Archives: 3; Jake Goldberg: 94 top; Grand Portage National Monument: 76, 87 right; Library of Congress: 9, 12, 30, 34, 36 right, 38, 51, 53; Chlaus Lotscher: 18 bottom, 41, 45 top; Museum of the American Indian: 10, 28 left, 46, 48, 68, 69; National Archives: 6, 8, 15, 29, 40, 59, 74; Northwest Territories Archives: 26, 28 right, 31, 32, 33, 37 left and right, 57, 60–61, 62, 64, 79, 87 left, 88; Northwest Territories Tourism: 17, 42 bottom, 44, 47 bottom, 65, 67, 71 bottom, 72, 89, 90, 92 bottom, 93, 94 bottom; Dan Polin: 24; Provincial Archives of Alberta/E. Brown Collection: 13, 36 left, 80; George Robbins: 82; Chase Roe: 91 bottom; Eda Rogers: 27; Rob Simpson: 16; Scott T. Smith: 18 top, 19, 20 top, 21, 22, 23 top; SuperStock: 20 bottom, 23 bottom; Voyageurs National Park: 47 top, 66.